Chaoyue 超越 Workbook: Advancin

Practice for Intermediate and Preadvanced Students

Authors:

Meng Yeh
France Yufen Lee Mehta
Mei-Ju Hwang
Yuanchao Meng
Natasha Pierce
Yea-Fen Chen

Illustrator: Amanda Wood

Columbia University Press
New York

Columbia University Press wishes to express its appreciation for assistance given by the Cultural Division of the Taipei Economic and Cultural Office in New York in the publication of this book.

Columbia University Press
Publishers Since 1893
New York   Chichester, West Sussex
Copyright © 2010 Cultural Division, Taipei Economic and Cultural Office in New York
All rights reserved

Library of Congress Cataloging-in-Publication Data
Chaoyue workbook : advancing in Chinese : practice for intermediate and preadvanced students / Yeh Meng ... [et al.] ; illustrated by Amanda Wood.
    p. cm.
Workbook to accompany: Chaoyue: advancing in Chinese.
Includes index.
ISBN 978-0-231-15623-3 (pbk.)
1. Chinese language--Textbooks for foreign speakers--English. I. Ye, Meng, 1950- II. Title.

PL1129.E5C385 2010
495.1'82421--dc22

2009006449

Contents

Lesson Three 新學期（新学期）

Lesson Four 職業與愛好（职业与爱好）

Lesson Eight 年輕人的網路世界（年轻人的网络世界）

Lesson Nine 複習（复习）

Lesson Ten 迎新春（迎新春）

Lesson Eleven 娛樂與藝術（娱乐与艺术）

Lesson Twelve 從四合院到摩天大樓（从四合院到摩天大楼）

Lesson Thirteen 留學（留学）

Lesson Fourteen 四海神遊（四海神游）

Lesson Fifteen 海外華人（海外华人）

Lesson Sixteen 保護瀕臨絕種的動物（保护濒临绝种的动物）

Lesson Seventeen 我們只有一個地球（我们只有一个地球）

Lesson Eighteen 複習（复习）

Introduction

The *Chaoyue* workbook provides ample performance-based tasks that students must complete by using the Chinese language in interpersonal, interpretive and presentational modes. Many of the exercises are similar to the questions in the AP Chinese Language and Culture exam. A number of tasks and projects require students to work together and conduct research in order to present their findings, conclusions, solutions or opinions. The workbook also includes exercises to strengthen students' understanding of vocabulary and sentence patterns in context. In addition, the *Chaoyue* workbook offers two simulated AP Chinese exams.

The workbook exercises for each lesson are divided into two sections, following the structure of the textbook lessons. The exercises are developed with the consideration of constantly recycling words learned previously. The various types of exercises are described below.

Vocabulary and Structure Exercises
The purpose of these exercises is to familiarize students with the new words and structures in each lesson. A variety of exercises, situated in relevant contexts, ask for students to match definitions, synonyms, and antonyms; complete sentences and paragraphs; classify words under categories; and list the advantages and disadvantages of certain practices.

Communicative Exercises
The communicative exercises in each lesson require students to use their speaking, reading, listening, and writing skills to complete the assignments in three communication modes. The communicative exercises include the following.

Exercise Type	Communication Mode	Examples
Listening	interpretive	• simple rejoinder • listening to an announcement, report, instruction, story, phone message
Listening and Writing	interpretive, presentational	writing down the key points for someone after listening to a phone message, announcement, or instruction
Reading	interpretive	• authentic ad, sign, flyer, brochure • letter, article, note, story, report
Reading and Writing	interpretive, presentational	responding to a letter or note in written format
Speaking	interpersonal	• listening and responding to questions orally • describing drawings orally
Writing	presentational	• describing a series of drawings • explaining, persuading, describing, comparing, and contrasting, narrating

Classroom Activities	interpretive, interpersonal, presentational	individual, small group or large group work that involve all three communication modes, such as • role-playing an interview • writing and performing a play • debating an issue • conducting a survey • planning a trip itinerary • organizing an event • designing a brochure • giving a short speech

Simulated AP Chinese Exams

Two simulated AP Chinese exams are provided in conjunction with review lessons 9 and 18 of the textbook. The format follows the AP exam, with multiple choices (listening and reading) and free responses (speaking and writing). The contents of the exams are related to the materials covered in the textbook lessons.

第一課　暑假、打工

第一课　暑假、打工

1.1. 暑假

1.1.1. 生詞練習（生词练习）

A. 夏令營的活動（夏令营的活动）: Check the activities that are likely to be included in an outdoor summer camp.

a. ❑補習數學（补习数学）		e. ❑釣魚（钓鱼）	
b. ❑爬山（爬山）		f. ❑考試（考试）	
c. ❑玩電腦（玩电脑）		g. ❑上網聊天（上网聊天）	
d. ❑餐廳打工（餐厅打工）		h. ❑騎馬（骑马）	

B. 填空: Here are Mark's comments about himself. Fill in the appropriate words below to complete the paragraph.

> 成熟，輕鬆，旅行，長大，經驗，準備
>
> 成熟，轻松，旅行，长大，经验，准备
>
> ---
>
> 　　今年我就滿十八歲了，真的_____了，不再是個小孩了，我父母也這麼認爲。他們_____讓我自己一個人去臺灣_____。今年不是考試就是忙著打工、申請大學，暑假能去臺灣是一個_____一下的好機會。而且這個_____也能讓我自己更_____。
>
> ★ ★ ★ ★ ★
>
> 　　今年我就满十八岁了，真的_____了，不再是个小孩了，我父母也这么认为。他们_____让我自己一个人去台湾_____。今年不是考试就是忙着打工、申请大学，暑假能去台湾是一个_____一下的好机会。而且这个_____也能让我自己更_____。

C. 完成句子: Choose an appropriate word below to complete each of the following sentences.

輕鬆，成熟，無聊，充實，棒極了
轻松，成熟，无聊，充实，棒极了

a.(   ) 李明今年暑假在夏令營當輔導員，每天都有很多事情
做，學到了很多東西，所以覺得很…
李明今年暑假在夏令营当辅导员，每天都有很多事情
做，学到了很多东西，所以觉得很…

b.(   ) 林文萍今年整個暑假都在上課，她覺得很沒有意思，非常…
林文萍今年整个暑假都在上课，她觉得很没有意思，非常…

c.(   ) 珍妮七月到歐洲旅行，去了德國、法國和西班牙，這次
旅行是她最難忘的假期，她覺得今年暑假…
珍妮七月到欧洲旅行，去了德国、法国和西班牙，这次
旅行是她最难忘的假期，她觉得今年暑假…

d.(   ) 有了在夏令營當輔導員的經驗，張大為覺得自己長大
了，比以前…
有了在夏令营当辅导员的经验，张大为觉得自己长大
了，比以前…

e.(   ) 剛考完試，又沒有功課，可以去看看電影，小梅覺得很…
刚考完试，又没有功课，可以去看看电影，小梅觉得很…

1.1.2. 聽力（听力）: Listen to the conversations and complete the rejoinders. You
will hear two short conversations or parts of conversations followed by four
choices, designated (A), (B), (C), and (D). Choose the one that continues or
completes the conversation in a logical and culturally appropriate manner.

1. (   ) 2. (   )

1.1.3. 短文閱讀 （短文阅读）： Wang Hong and Mary each wrote a short description of their summer vacations. Based on their notes, use English to fill in the information in the form to show how Wang Hong and Mary spent their summer.

王紅和瑪莉的暑假

王紅的暑假

今年暑假我在加州參加了四個星期的中文夏令營。那兒的輔導員帶我們參加活動時都只說中文，而且活動也都跟中華文化有關：武術、寫毛筆字什麼的。我們每天吃道地的中國菜，在販賣部買零食也得用中文。在那兒時間過得很快，也很充實。剛開始，我根本聽不懂輔導員說的話，但是一個星期以後就慢慢聽懂了。這四個星期從早到晚都在說中文的環境裏，對提高我的中文能力有很大的幫助。有了這個經驗後我更想到中國去旅行了，希望明年有機會。

★ ★ ★ ★ ★

瑪莉的暑假

今年暑假過得棒極了！我和哥哥兩個人去加拿大的西北部爬山、露營了兩個星期。父母剛開始有點擔心，但是哥哥已經很大了，他跟爸爸媽媽說他能夠負責我的安全，會好好照顧我。我們每天為了看日出都起得很早，下午除了爬山還經常去釣魚，晚上吃的大多是自己釣的魚。最後一晚最棒，營地只剩下我們，偶爾聽到動物的聲音，其他聲音都沒有，只有天上數不清的星星。以前我認爲露營最無聊，不能看電視，也不能上網。但是現在我成熟多了，沒有那些東西也可以過得很輕鬆快樂。

	what she did	how she feels about the experience	the impact of the experience
Wang Hong			
Mary			

王红的暑假

今年暑假我在加州参加了四个星期的中文夏令营。那儿的辅导员带我们参加活动时都只说中文，而且活动也都跟中华文化有关：武术、写毛笔字什么的。我们每天吃道地的中国菜，在贩卖部买零食也得用中文。在那儿时间过得很快，也很充实。刚开始，我根本听不懂辅导员说的话，但是一个星期以后就慢慢听懂了。这四个星期从早到晚都在说中文的环境里，对提高我的中文能力有很大的帮助。有了这个经验后我更想到中国去旅行了，希望明年有机会。

★★★★★

玛莉的暑假

今年暑假过得棒极了！我和哥哥两个人去加拿大的西北部爬山、露营了两个星期。父母刚开始有点担心，但是哥哥已经很大了，他跟爸爸妈妈说他能够负责我的安全，会好好照顾我。我们每天为了看日出都起得很早，下午除了爬山还经常去钓鱼，晚上吃的大多是自己钓的鱼。最后一晚最棒，营地只剩下我们，偶尔听到动物的声音，其他声音都没有，只有天上数不清的星星。以前我认为露营最无聊，不能看电视，也不能上网。但是现在我成熟多了，没有那些东西也可以过得很轻松快乐。

	what she did	how she feels about the experience	the impact of the experience
Wang Hong			
Mary			

1.1.4. 口語回答（口语回答）：For the speech sample, you will need to answer six questions. After you hear each question, you have twenty seconds to record your response. For each question, you should respond as fully and as appropriately as possible.

1.1.5. 課堂口語活動（课堂口语活动）

A. 李華的暑假（李华的暑假）：

B. 你的暑假: Describe your last summer vacation. Choose one of the most interesting activities to present with photos taken during the summer.

1.1.6. 寫作（写作）

A. Plan your summer vacation after you graduate in May next year. What would you like to do before you head to college? Write a paragraph including the details of your plan and explain why you want to do those activities. Use the words in the box in your writing.

| 另，而且，經驗，假期，機會，準備，參加 |
| 另，而且，经验，假期，机会，准备，参加 |

B. Describe one of your worst summer vacations. If you have a chance to take the same vacation again, what would you do differently?

1.2. 打工經驗（打工经验）

1.2.1. 生詞練習（生词练习）

A. 連連看（连连看）: Match the employee on the left with the place on the right where he or she more likely works.

a. 職員（职员）	游泳池
b. 救生員（救生员）	速食店
c. 店員（店员）	夏令營（夏令营）
d. 輔導員（辅导员）	銀行（银行）
e. 服務生（服务生）	商店

B. 解釋 [1] 生詞（解释 [1] 生词）: **a** to **f** are definitions for the words in the box. Find and fill in the appropriate word for each definition.

> 小費，校園，義工，零用錢，工資，存錢
> 小费，校园，义工，零用钱，工资，存钱

a. （   ）　　幫忙工作，不拿薪水
　　　　　　　　帮忙工作，不拿薪水

b. （   ）　　把錢放在銀行裏
　　　　　　　　把钱放在银行里

c. （   ）　　顧客給服務生的錢，不是薪水
　　　　　　　　顾客给服务生的钱，不是薪水

d. （   ）　　在學校裏(在学校里)

e. （   ）　　工作所賺的錢
　　　　　　　　工作所赚的钱

f. （   ）　　爸媽每個星期給你去看電影、買東西的錢。
　　　　　　　　爸妈每个星期给你去看电影、买东西的钱。

---

[1] 解釋（解释）[ㄐㄧㄝˇㄕˋ, jiěshì] *to explain*

C. 填空: Fill in appropriate words from the list to complete the following two paragraphs.

a. David is talking about his part-time job during the summer.

負責，參加，另，當，照顧，活動
负责，参加，另，当，照顾，活动

今年暑假我在一個養老院_____義工。我很喜歡這個經驗，因爲我喜歡跟那些老爺爺、老奶奶一起_____很多有意思的_____。_____一個原因是我得_____他們的安全、_____他們的生活，所以我覺得自己也成熟多了。

★★★★★

今年暑假我在一个养老院_____义工。我很喜欢这个经验，因为我喜欢跟那些老爷爷、老奶奶一起_____很多有意思的_____。_____一个原因是我得_____他们的安全、_____他们的生活，所以我觉得自己也成熟多了。

b. Tiantian met Lisa on campus yesterday and learned about Lisa's summer.

存錢，一直，小費，辛苦，碰到，薪水，服務生，店員
存钱，一直，小费，辛苦，碰到，薪水，服务生，店员

我昨天在校園_____莉莎。她暑假白天在商店當_____，晚上是餐廳的_____。餐廳工作的_____不高，但是有很多_____。可是工作很_____，從五點_____工作到十點，不能休息。莉莎這麼努力賺錢是因爲她得_____上大學。

★ ★ ★ ★ ★

我昨天在校园_____莉莎。她暑假白天在商店当_____，晚上是餐厅的_____。餐厅工作的_____不高，但是有很多_____。可是工作很_____，从五点_____工作到十点，不能休息。莉莎这么努力赚钱是因为她得_____上大学。

1.2.2. 聽力（听力）

A. You will hear a conversation between a male student and a female student regarding their summer camp experiences. Listen to the recording and check the appropriate box that reflects the experiences of the male student and the female student.

女 男

a. ☐☐ Went to Taiwan to visit grandparents

b. ☐☐ Worked at a summer camp and was responsible for children's safety

c. ☐☐ Taught English to little children

d. ☐☐ Worked at a fast food restaurant

e. ☐☐ Gained some teaching experience

f. ☐☐ Made a new friend at the summer camp

g. ☐☐ Interested in being a teacher in the future

h. ☐☐ Wants to take driving lessons

B. Listen to the conversations and complete the rejoinders. You will hear two short conversations or parts of conversations followed by four choices, designated (A), (B), (C), and (D). Choose the one that continues or completes the conversation in a logical and culturally appropriate manner.

1. (　　) 2. (　　)

1.2.3. 短文閱讀（短文阅读）： Based on the short reading, answer the following four questions.

Xiaofang is spending summer vacation with her parents back in Taiwan. She is sending an e-mail to her cousin in the United States.

表妹：

今年暑假我和父母回到臺灣看爺爺、奶奶，偶爾教教鄰居的小孩一點英語，可以得到經驗又可以賺點零用錢，而且幫小朋友補習英文對我來說也根本不是問題，很輕鬆。我想存點錢，將來也許有機會買車或是去旅行。速食店的工作怎麼樣？週末還一直在游泳池當救生員嗎？

小芳

★ ★ ★ ★ ★

表妹：

今年暑假我和父母回到台湾看爷爷、奶奶，偶尔教教邻居的小孩一点英语，可以得到经验又可以赚点零用钱，而且帮小朋友补习英文对我来说也根本不是问题，很轻松。我想存点钱，将来也许有机会买车或去旅行。快餐店的工作怎么样？周末还一直在游泳池当救生员吗？

小芳

---

a. 你想小芳的父母是什麼地方人？
   你想小芳的父母是什么地方人？

b. 為什麼小芳覺得幫小朋友補習英文對她來說不是問題？
   为什么小芳觉得帮小朋友补习英文对她来说不是问题？

c. 小芳計劃怎麼用她暑假打工賺的錢？
   小芳计划怎么用她暑假打工赚的钱？

d. 小芳的表妹暑假在哪兒打工？
   小芳的表妹暑假在哪儿打工？

1.2.4. 閱讀短文（阅读短文）

招聘請人

本公司水上樂園遊樂區急聘暑期工讀生。
十六歲以上高中學生，工作認真，成熟負責。
一星期工作三十小時，每小時付臺幣兩百元。

意者請於五月十日前將履歷表寄至：台中縣大
富鄉北村通達路 81 號　李先生收。

★ ★ ★ ★ ★

招聘请人

本公司水上乐园游乐区急聘暑期工读生。
十六岁以上高中学生，工作认真，成熟负责。
一星期工作三十小时，每小时付台币两百元。

意者请于五月十日前将履历表寄至：台中县大
富乡北村通达路 81 号　李先生收。

Answer the following questions in English based on the reading above.

    a. What kind of information is provided?

    b. What are the criteria for applying for the job?

    c. What does the job offer?

    d. How do you apply for the job?

1.2.5. 課堂口語活動（课堂口语活动）

A. Debating: should high school students concentrate only on studying or should they also have a part-time job during the school year?

B. In addition to the part-time jobs mentioned in lesson 1, research and find out what other kinds of part-time jobs are available for high school students. Give a short presentation of the job that you choose, and give your opinion about whether it is a job worth applying for.

1.2.6. 看圖寫作（看图写作）

The four pictures tell a story. Imagine you are writing the story to a friend. Narrate a complete story as suggested by the pictures. Give your story a beginning, a middle part, and an end.

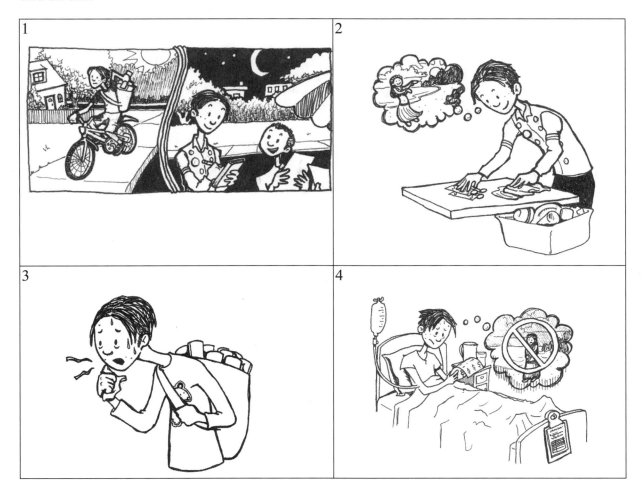

1.2.7. 寫作 （写作）

A. Write a letter to apply for the job advertised in 1.2.4 and explain why you are interested and well qualified.

B. Describe the ideal summer job or volunteer experience that you would like to have in the future: What responsibilities would you take on? What would you gain in terms of wages, experience, and knowledge learned? How would it benefit you in the future? Try to include the vocabulary provided in the box.

> 成熟，輕鬆，旅行，長大了，經驗，準備，負責，參加，另，
> 當，照顧，活動
>
> 成熟，轻松，旅行，长大了，经验，准备，负责，参加，另，
> 当，照顾，活动

第二課　　交朋友

第二課　　交朋友

2.1. 好朋友

2.1.1. 生詞練習（生词练习）

A. 連連看（连连看）： Match the vocabulary with the description.

a. 自信	學東西學得很快（学东西学得很快）
b. 聰明（聪明）	很多事情都不怕（很多事情都不怕）
c. 文靜（文静）	注意到很多小地方（注意到很多小地方）
d. 細心（细心）	兩個人的興趣相同（两个人的兴趣相同）
e. 外表	能力很強（能力很强）
f. 隨和（随和）	對自己很有信心（对自己很有信心）
g. 勇敢	很容易跟人相處（很容易跟人相处）
h. 能幹（能干）	不為小事煩心（不为小事烦心）
i. 開朗（开朗）	不常說話（不常说话）
j. 志同道合	一個人長的樣子（一个人长的样子）

B. 外表？個性？（外表？个性？）： Do the adjectives in the following describe physical appearance or personality? Write either 外表 or 個性(个性)next to the adjective.

活潑（活泼）＿＿＿＿　　　壯（壮）＿＿＿＿　　　帥（帅）＿＿＿＿

細心（细心）＿＿＿＿　　　勇敢＿＿＿＿　　　矮＿＿＿＿

隨和（随和）＿＿＿＿　　　瘦＿＿＿＿　　　內向＿＿＿＿

C. 找筆友（找笔友）: You are looking for a pen pal with the same interests as yours. Provide your personal information in the form for the prospective pen pals.

姓名		性別 女　男	年齡 （年龄）	
外表	1.＿＿＿＿＿＿＿＿　　2.＿＿＿＿＿＿＿＿　　3.＿＿＿＿＿＿＿＿			
個性 （个性）	1.＿＿＿＿＿＿＿＿　　2.＿＿＿＿＿＿＿＿　　3.＿＿＿＿＿＿＿＿			
對什麼有興趣？（对什么有兴趣？） 1.＿＿＿＿＿＿＿＿＿＿＿＿＿　　　2.＿＿＿＿＿＿＿＿＿＿＿＿＿ 對什麼沒興趣？（对什么没兴趣？） 1.＿＿＿＿＿＿＿＿＿＿＿＿＿　　　2.＿＿＿＿＿＿＿＿＿＿＿＿＿				

2.1.2. 聽力（听力）

A. You will hear six descriptions, **a** to **f**. Match each of the descriptions with an appropriate picture by writing the letter in the box next to the picture.

B. Listen to the conversations and complete the rejoinders. You will hear two short conversations or parts of conversations followed by four choices, designated (A), (B), (C), and (D). Choose the one that continues or completes the conversation in a logical and culturally appropriate manner.

1. (   )   2. (   )

2.1.3. 短文閱讀（短文阅读）： Li Yan is describing her best friend, Anna. After reading Li Yan's description, use English to fill in the information in the form for Anna and Li Yan.

李艷最好的朋友

　　我叫李艷。我最好的朋友名字叫安娜，她也住在波士頓，跟我一樣大，今年也上十二年級，但是我們不上同一個學校。她長得不高但是很壯，有著深咖啡色的短髮和咖啡色的眼睛，皮膚紅紅的。她常說她最喜歡我的黑色長髮和黑黑的皮膚。安娜很外向，喜歡運動，朋友也很多。雖然我不太愛說話，有點害羞，個性跟安娜不太一樣，但是我們從小一起長大，我們很談得來，也都喜歡上網聊天。

李艳最好的朋友

　　我叫李艳。我最好的朋友名字叫安娜，她也住在波士顿，跟我一样大，今年也上十二年级，但是我们不上同一个学校。她长得不高但是很壮，有着深咖啡色的短发和咖啡色的眼睛，皮肤红红的。她常说她最喜欢我的黑色长发和黑黑的皮肤。安娜很外向，喜欢运动，朋友也很多。虽然我不太爱说话，有点害羞，个性跟安娜不太一样，但是我们从小一起长大，我们很谈得来，也都喜欢上网聊天。

	Grade	Appearance	Personality
Anna			
Li Yan			

2.1.4. 口語回答（口语回答）: For this exercise, you will need to answer seven questions. After you hear each question, you have twenty seconds to record your response. For each question, you should respond as fully and as appropriately as possible.

2.1.5. 課堂口語活動（课堂口语活动）

A. 湯姆[1]和威廉[2]（汤姆和威廉）: Compare the physical looks and interests of Tom and William based on the drawings. Take a guess at their personalities too.

B. 你最喜歡的電影明星[3]、歌星[4]（你最喜欢的电影明星[1]、歌星[2]）: Describe your favorite movie star or singer—his or her looks, personality, and talents—and explain why you like him or her. Use a poster with photos.

---

[1] 湯姆（汤姆）[ㄊㄤ ㄇㄨˇ, Tāngmǔ] *Tom*

[2] 威廉 [ㄨㄟ ㄌㄧㄢˊ, Wēilián] *William*

[3] 明星 [ㄇㄧㄥˊ ㄒㄧㄥ, míngxīng] *movie star*

[4] 歌星 [ㄍㄜ ㄒㄧㄥ, gēxīng] *singer*

2.1.6. 寫作（写作）

A. 最要好的朋友: Write a short paragraph describing your best friend, including answers for the following questions.

> a. 你最好的朋友是誰？（你最好的朋友是谁？）
> b. 他/她長什麼樣子？（他/她长什么样子？）
> c. 他/她的個性怎麼樣？（他/她的个性怎么样？）

B. 個性報告（个性报告）: Below is a list of three different personalities. Think of the people around you such as your classmates, friends, or family members as examples. Write a short paragraph to describe each person, including an example to explain why the personality fits him or her.

個性（个性）：開放（开放），內向，活潑（活泼）

2.2. 交朋友

2.2.1. 生詞練習（生词练习）

A. 高中生交朋友: People have different opinions about high school dating. Based on your opinions, list the pros and cons in Chinese.

好處（好处）	壞處（坏处）

B. 反義詞（反义词）: Fill in an antonym, chosen from the list, for each of the following words.

> 存錢，在一起，分心，不明白，很輕鬆，高興，很長時間，合不來
> 存钱，在一起，分心，不明白，很轻松，高兴，很长时间，合不来

a. _____ 專心（专心）

b. _____ 轉眼之間（转眼之间）

c. _____ 浪費（浪费）

d. _____ 傷心（伤心）

e. _____ 瞭解（了解）

f. _____ 壓力大（压力大）

g. _____ 談得來（谈得来）

C. 填空: Mike and Miss Wang have views on dating in high school, which are stated in the following paragraphs **a** and **b**. Fill in the appropriate words from the list to complete the two paragraphs.

經驗，分手，壓力，機會，浪費時間，專心讀書，瞭解女孩
经验，分手，压力，机会，浪费时间，专心读书，了解女孩

a.

麥克，十七歲，高中生

　　雖然我已經十七歲了，也有很多很好的女的朋友，但是我從來沒有交女朋友的＿＿＿＿＿＿，因為我爸媽覺得我還太小，交女朋友太＿＿＿＿＿＿，應該要先＿＿＿＿＿＿，不然上不了好的大學。可是我覺得高中的時候交女朋友可以幫助我們＿＿＿＿＿＿，沒有什麼不好。

麦克，十七岁，高中生

　　虽然我已经十七岁了，也有很多很好的女的朋友，但是我从来没有交女朋友的＿＿＿＿＿＿，因为我爸妈觉得我还太小，交女朋友太＿＿＿＿＿＿，应该要先＿＿＿＿＿＿，不然上不了好的大学。可是我觉得高中的时候交女朋友可以帮助我们＿＿＿＿＿＿，没有什么不好。

b.

王小姐，二十二歲，大學生

　　以前由於爸媽給我的＿＿＿＿＿＿，我跟我高中的那個男朋友＿＿＿＿＿＿了。雖然現在上了大學也有很多＿＿＿＿＿＿，但是我還是覺得以前在高中時候的男朋友最好，無論什麼時候我都想到他。

王小姐，二十二岁，大学生

　　以前由于爸妈给我的＿＿＿＿＿＿，我跟我高中的那个男朋友＿＿＿＿＿＿了。虽然现在上了大学也有很多＿＿＿＿＿＿，但是我还是觉得以前在高中时候的男朋友最好，无论什么时候我都想到他。

2.2.2. 聽力（听力）

A. You will hear a phone message left for your friend Xiao Zhang. Please relay the message to Xiao Zhang in a written note.

B. Listen to the conversations and complete the rejoinders. You will hear two short conversations or parts of conversations followed by four choices, designated (A), (B), (C), and (D). Choose the one that continues or completes the conversation in a logical and culturally appropriate manner.

1. (   )   2. (   )

2.2.3. 閱讀短文（阅读短文）： Wang Xiaomei wrote an e-mail back to Kaili. Based on the e-mail, answer the following questions.

凱莉：

我的暑假過得還可以，沒去什麼地方玩，大部分時間都在補習英文和數學。開學後我就高三了，得好好準備高考。 我爸媽也一樣，覺得在高中不應該交男朋友、浪費時間。我也沒什麼機會認識男孩子。代我問候 Chris。你們有機會再見面嗎？

小梅

凱莉：

我的暑假过得还可以，没去什麼地方玩，大部分时间都在补习英文和数学。开学后我就高三了，得好好准备高考。 我爸妈也一样，觉得在高中不应该交男朋友、浪费时间。 我也没什麼机会认识男孩子。 代我问候 Chris。你们有机会再见面吗？

小梅

---

a. 小梅覺得她的暑假過得怎麼樣？
   小梅觉得她的暑假过得怎么样？

b. 暑假期間王小梅做什麼？王小梅去什麼地方玩了？
   暑假期间王小梅做什么？王小梅去什么地方玩了？

c. 小梅的父母讓她在高中交男朋友嗎？爲什麼？
   小梅的父母让她在高中交男朋友吗？为什么？

2.2.4. 實文閱讀（实文阅读）： Read the authentic ad below and choose the correct answers for the following questions.

徵友啟事

姓名：王心

年齡：25 歲

性別：女

學歷：大學畢業

外表：高高瘦瘦（身高 178 公分，體重 55 公斤）

個性：內向、文靜、細心、隨和

興趣：看書、聽音樂、旅行

要求：年齡、學歷、興趣相近，聰明、能幹、幽默的人

意者請電郵：xinwang@chaoyue.com

征友启事

姓名：王心

年龄：25 岁

性别：女

学历：大学毕业

外表：高高瘦瘦（身高 178 公分，体重 55 公斤）

个性：内向、文静、细心、随和

兴趣：看书、听音乐、旅行

要求：年龄、学历、兴趣相近，聪明、能干、幽默的人

意者请电邮：xinwang@chaoyue.com

---

a. What kind of information is provided?
1) school name
2) home address
3) description of her appearance

b. What kind of friends is she looking for?
1) middle-aged
2) capable
3) very outgoing

c. What is her hobby?
1) traveling
2) eating Chinese food
3) chatting with friends

2.2.5. 課堂口語活動（课堂口语活动）

A. A group of students from China are visiting your high school. They are interested in many aspects of high school life in the United States, especially dating. Your class is assigned to give the group a presentation titled "Dating in American High Schools." Discuss in small groups as to what should be included in the presentation that will provide the most accurate information on this topic.

B. In small groups, discuss the advice regarding dating in high schools that you can give to your fellow classmates. Each group should present its advice and explain the importance of the advice.

2.2.6. 看圖寫作（看图写作）: The four pictures tell a story. Imagine you are writing the story to a friend. Narrate the complete story as suggested by the pictures. Give your story a beginning, a middle part, and an end.

2.2.7. 寫作（写作）

A. Your parents have forbidden you to date while in high school. Write a persuasive letter to change their mind.

B. Ask your parents if they had the experience of dating in high school and what their opinions about dating in high school are. Based on the interview with your parents, write a paragraph.

第三課　　新學期
第三课　　新学期

3.1. 高中課程、社團（高中课程、社团）

3.1.1. 生詞練習（生词练习）

A. 下面這些科目哪些是文科？哪些是理科？Write either 文科 or 理科 next to the subjects.

a. 數學（数学）＿＿＿＿＿　　f. 物理　　　　＿＿＿＿＿

b. 歷史（历史）＿＿＿＿＿　　g. 地理　　　　＿＿＿＿＿

c. 英文　　　　＿＿＿＿＿　　h. 戲劇（戏剧）＿＿＿＿＿

d. 化學（化学）＿＿＿＿＿　　i. 藝術（艺术）＿＿＿＿＿

e. 中文　　　　＿＿＿＿＿　　j. 生物　　　　＿＿＿＿＿

B. 下面這些活動哪些是社團活動？（下面这些活动哪些是社团活动？）：
Check the activities that belong to the category of after-school activities.

a. ❑合唱練習（合唱练习）

b. ❑寫文學報告（写文学报告）

c. ❑選大學先修課（选大学先修课）

d. ❑製作畢業紀念冊（制作毕业纪念册）

e. ❑樂隊演奏（乐队演奏）

f. ❑上美國政治課（上美国政治课）

g. ❑幫校刊攝影（帮校刊摄影）

h. ❑學圍棋（学围棋）

i. ❑唱卡拉 OK

j. ❑辯論比賽（辩论比赛）

C. 選一選（选一选）: Choose an appropriate definition from the right column to define each of the words in the left column.

_____大學先修課　　　　　a. 互相比較，看誰最好
　　　大学先修课　　　　　　　 互相比较，看谁最好

_____擅長　　　　　　　　b. 放學以後所做的活動
　　　擅长　　　　　　　　　　 放学以后所作的活动

_____課外活動　　　　　　c. 興趣相同的人組成的團體
　　　课外活动　　　　　　　　 兴趣相同的人组成的团体

_____社團　　　　　　　　d. 計畫
　　　社团　　　　　　　　　　 计划

_____嚴格　　　　　　　　e. 特別好的技術
　　　严格　　　　　　　　　　 特别好的技术

_____競爭　　　　　　　　f. 一定要學的科目
　　　竞争　　　　　　　　　　 一定要学的科目

_____必修課　　　　　　　g. 給高中生上的大學課程
　　　必修课　　　　　　　　　 给高中生上的大学课程

_____打算　　　　　　　　h. 不放鬆，不馬虎
　　　打算　　　　　　　　　　 不放松，不马虎

3.1.2. 聽力 （听力）: You will hear two announcements made by a school counselor on the school intercom. Listen to each of the announcements and select the correct answers for the following questions.

1. What is the main message of the first announcement?
   a. Every student should have four credits of foreign language before graduation.
   b. The school will add Japanese starting this year.
   c. The school offers five elective foreign languages this semester.
   d. Four foreign language credits are required to enter this high school.

2. What is also mentioned in the second announcement?
   a. The school will offer after-class tutoring for three subjects.
   b. The school will offer a biology AP course next year.
   c. Students should consult with Teacher Huang regarding AP courses.
   d. Students should arrange tutoring hours through Teacher Huang.

3.1.3. 短文閱讀（短文阅读）： School has just started. Xiaoli, a senior at a high school in Massachusetts, exchanges e-mails with Meiling, a cousin who lives in California. Read their e-mails and fill in the chart in English.

Xiaoli's e-mail to Meiling

美玲：

你好！開學了嗎？我們已經開始上課了。這學期我選了六門課，物理、英文和數學都是必修課，另外還選了大學中文先修課、藝術和音樂。物理和數學課很無聊，老師又嚴格，第一天上課就給了很多功課，我真不喜歡這兩門課。大學中文先修課很有趣，老師要我們常常上網看中文，用電腦[1]寫作業。這學期我參加了辯論社，還被選爲辯論社的社長。辯論社的同學每個星期四下午一起練習辯論不同的題目。這個學期我們會在三所高中比賽三場。這學期雖然必修科目沒有那麼多，但是大家都得忙著準備申請大學。你選了什麼課？參加什麼社團了嗎？請回信。

小莉

★ ★ ★ ★ ★

美玲：

你好！开学了吗？我们已经开始上课了。这学期我选了六门课，物理、英文和数学都是必修课，另外还选了大学中文先修课、艺术和音乐。物理和数学课很无聊，老师又严格，第一天上课就给了很多功课，我真不喜欢这两门课。大学中文先修课很有趣，老师要我们常常上网看中文，用计算机[1]写作业。这学期我参加了辩论社，还被选为辩论社的社长。辩论社的同学每个星期四下午一起练习辩论不同的题目。这个学期我们会在三所高中比赛三场。这学期虽然必修科目没有那么多，但是大家都得忙着准备申请大学。你选了什么课？参加社团什么社团了吗？请回信。

小莉

---

[1] 電腦 [ㄉㄧㄢˋㄋㄠˇ, diànnǎo] *computer (Taiwan)*；計算機 [ㄐㄧˋㄙㄨㄢˋㄐㄧ, jìsuànjī] *computer (PRC)*

小莉：

你好！我們已經上了一星期的課了。這學期我只要選英文和物理這兩門必修課就可以畢業了。我也選了大學法文先修課，要是考得好，就可以直接選大學三年級的法文，太棒了！高中最後一年終於可以選自己真正喜歡的課了。我選了政治、戲劇、藝術。這三門課又輕鬆又有趣，老師也不那麼嚴格。今年我參加了攝影社，交了很多喜歡拍照的朋友，我還是畢業紀念冊的攝影師呢！日子過得真快，我們馬上就要申請大學了。祝你學業進步。

美玲

★ ★ ★ ★ ★

小莉：

你好！我们已经上了一星期的课了。这学期我只要选英文和物理这两门必修课就可以毕业了。我也选了大学法文先修课，要是考得好，就可以直接选大学三年级的法文，太棒了！高中最后一年终于可以选自己真正喜欢的课了。我选了政治、戏剧、艺术。这三门课又轻松又有趣，老师也不那么严格。今年我参加了摄影社，交了很多喜欢拍照的朋友，我还是毕业纪念册的摄影师呢！日子过得真快，我们马上就要申请大学了。祝你学业进步。

美玲

Based on the e-mails, fill in answers to the following questions in English.

	Xiaoli	Meiling
Which required courses do they take?		
How do they feel about their required courses?		
Which elective courses do they take ?		
How do they feel about their elective courses?		
What club do they belong to?		
What do they do at their club?		

3.1.4. 口語回答（口语回答）: For the speech sample, you will need to answer seven questions. After you hear each question, you will have twenty seconds to record your response. For each question, you should respond as fully and as appropriately as possible.

3.1.5. 課堂口語活動（课堂口语活动）

A. 看圖說話（看图说话）

Mark is the president of the Chinese Club at school. He introduces the club and its activities this semester during new-student orientation.

B. It is the beginning of the semester. All the school's clubs would like to recruit new members. Each of you (or each small group) represents a club. Introduce the activities that the club has planned and encourage students to participate. Each student (or small group) can choose from the current existing school clubs or can create one.

3.1.6. 寫作（写作）

A. Write a letter to your pen pal in China, telling him or her the classes you are taking and the clubs you are in. Also include any school news that you think is worth knowing. Use words from the box in your writing. Ask your pen pal about his or her new semester.

科目，課外活動，課業，理科，選，學分，必修課，選修課
科目，课外活动，课业，理科，选，学分，必修课，选修课

B. An exchange student from a sister school in Taiwan will spend one semester at your high school in the spring. You are the host for this student. Write a letter to him or her, introducing yourself and telling him or her what classes, clubs, and after-school activities your school offers. You also need to make some suggestions about courses to take and clubs to join, as well as provide any information that you think he or she should be aware of.

3.2. 高中生活（高中生活）

3.2.1. 生詞練習 （生词练习）

A. 完成句子: Complete each sentence by using the words provided. The sentence in **a** has already been completed as an example.

   a. 課外活動和課業並重…申請…
      课外活动和课业并重…申请…

      課外活動和課業並重對申請大學很有幫助。
      课外活动和课业并重对申请大学很有帮助。

   b. 明年五月就要畢業了…把握…
      明年五月就要毕业了…把握…

   c. 當學校報紙記者…收穫…
      当学校报纸记者…收获…

   d. 我這學期修了五門必修課…對…有興趣…
      我这学期修了五门必修课…对…有兴趣…

   e. 在中國能不能上大學…就看…
      在中国能不能上大学…就看…

B. 解釋生詞（解释生词）: **a** to **g** are definitions for the words in the box. Find and fill in the appropriate word for each definition.

> 並重，記者，激烈，課業，感想，收穫，麻煩
> 并重，记者，激烈，课业，感想，收获，麻烦

   a.(   ) 經過工作、努力所得到的（经过工作、努力所得到的）
   b.(   ) 在學校的學習（在学校的学习）
   c.(   ) 兩個都一樣重要（两个都一样重要）
   d.(   ) 事情發生以後的想法（事情发生以后的想法）
   e.(   ) 很難、不容易（很难、不容易）
   f.(   ) 很大、很強的反應（很大、很强的反应）
   g.(   ) 採訪新聞的人（采访新闻的人）

C. 填空： Nina and David are twelfth graders starting this year. They are sharing with each other their classes, activities, and ideas. Fill in appropriate words from the list to complete the following two paragraphs.

a. Nina is talking about her new school year.

> 激烈，畢業，壓力，課業，記者，採訪，嚴格
> 激烈，毕业，压力，课业，记者，采访，严格

今年我選了四門必修課，這四門都是理科，每一門的
_____都很困難，老師很_____，同學間的競爭又
_____，對我來說_____真的很大。而且，這學期我
是校刊的_____，得_____明年五月要_____的
同學，所以課外活動的壓力也不小。

★ ★ ★ ★ ★

今年我选了四门必修课，这四门都是理科，每一门的
_____都很困难，老师很_____，同学间的竞争又
_____，对我来说_____真的很大。而且，这学期我
是校刊的_____，得_____明年五月要_____的
同学，所以课外活动的压力也不小。

b. David is talking about his new school year to Nina.

加油，收穫，擅長，困難，課程，把握，幫助
加油，收获，擅长，困难，课程，把握，帮助

　　我最_____的科目是生物，因此這學期選了生物的大學先修課。這門課有點兒 _____，可是可以_____我準備大學的_____。我還參加了學校啦啦隊 (cheer team)，要是有美式足球賽或者籃球比賽，我們就得去_____。我希望能好好 _____高中最後一年，得到更多的 _____。

★ ★ ★ ★ ★

　　我最_____的科目是生物，因此这学期选了生物的大学先修课。这门课有点儿 _____，可是可以_____我准备大学的_____。我还参加了学校啦啦队 (cheer team)，要是有美式足球赛或者篮球比赛，我们就得去_____。我希望能好好 _____高中最后一年，得到更多的 _____。

3.2.2. 聽力（听力）

A. During the assembly at the beginning of each year, the president of each club gives a short speech about the club. In the following, you will hear such a short speech.

    a. What club is mentioned in the speech?
        1) Biology Club   2) Science Club   3) Nature Club

    b. What kind of activity by the club is planned in November?
        1) camping   2) going to a lake   3) going to a seashore

    c. What is the qualification to participate in the club?
        1) One should have taken biology and chemistry courses.
        2) One needs to have an interview with Teacher Li.
        3) One has to maintain a B average grade point.

    d. What is the activity held on campus?
        1) doing various experiments
        2) holding contests
        3) listening to the lectures given by Teacher Li

B. Listen to the conversations and complete the rejoinders. You will hear two short conversations or parts of conversations followed by four choices, designated (A), (B), (C), and (D). Choose the one that continues or completes the conversation in a logical and culturally appropriate manner.

1. (　) 　 2. (　)

3.2.3. 閱讀、寫作（阅读、写作）： Zhigao, your Chinese pen pal, wrote you the following e-mail. Write an e-mail to respond.

你開學了嗎？我這幾個星期都睡得不夠。為了準備高考，天天開夜車，每天上完課後還得補習。你每天花多少時間念書啊？我知道你們除了讀書，還有很多社團活動。這學期你參加了什麼社團？我很想瞭解你們有哪些活動，在社團裏做什麼？另外，聽說在美國高中，畢業舞會是一件大事。你覺得呢？打算請誰？你跳舞跳得怎麼樣？我一點也不會，到現在都還沒參加過舞會呢！

志高

★ ★ ★ ★ ★

你开学了吗？我这几个星期都睡得不够。为了准备高考，天天开夜车，每天上完课后还得补习。你每天花多少时间念书啊？我知道你们除了读书，还有很多社团活动。这学期你参加了什么社团？我很想了解你们有哪些活动，在社团里做什么。另外，听说在美国高中，毕业舞会是一件大事，你觉得呢？打算请谁？你跳舞跳得怎么样？我一点也不会，到现在还没参加过舞会呢！

志高

3.2.4. 實文閱讀（实文阅读）： The following flyer announces a Go competition. Answer the following questions based upon the information provided.

圍棋比賽

比賽時間： 十月八日，星期六上午九點
比賽地點： 春田市立圖書館二樓
報名資格： 老少不拘，有興趣人士一概歡迎
報名組別： 小學組，國中組，高中組，成人組
報名日期： 九月五日起至九月三十日止
報名地點： 春田市立圖書館一樓

獎品： 第一名得數位攝影機一台和現金三百元
第二名得卡拉 OK 伴唱機一台和現金二百元
第三名得手機一支和現金一百元

歡迎大家踴躍報名

有問題請電：王小姐
xxx-866-0868，jj@chaoyue.com

★ ★ ★ ★ ★

围棋比赛

比赛时间： 十月八日，星期六上午九点
比赛地点： 春田市立图书馆二楼
报名资格： 老少不拘，有兴趣人士一概欢迎
报名组别： 小学组，国中组，高中组，成人组
报名日期： 九月五日起至九月三十日止
报名地点： 春田市立图书馆一楼

奖品： 第一名得数位摄影机一台和现金三百元
第二名得卡拉 OK 伴唱机一台和现金二百元
第三名得手机一支和现金一百元

欢迎大家踊跃报名

有问题请电：王小姐
xxx-866-0868，jj@chaoyue.com

a. When is the deadline for registration?
1) September 5   2) September 30   3) October 8   4) November 10

b. Which group is in the competition?
1) adults   2) college students   3) professionals   4) international students

c. Where is the competition going to be held?
1) middle school library, first floor
2) middle school library, second floor
3) city library, first floor
4) city library, second floor

d. What award will the champion win?
1) a luxury Go set
2) $200 cash
3) a digital camera
4) a karaoke player

3.2.5. 課堂口語活動（课堂口语活动）

A. You will have an interview as a requirement to be accepted into a prestigious college. Prepare a short speech to talk about the most interesting courses you have taken during your high school experience. You will also need to talk about your memorable experiences from any clubs or after-school activities.

B. Discuss the following two questions in small groups and present the group discussion.
  a. What kinds of courses a student should take during his or her senior year and why.
  b. Your "ideal" senior prom.

3.2.6. 看圖寫作（看图写作）: The four pictures tell a story. Imagine you are writing the story to a friend. Narrate a complete story as suggested by the pictures. Give your story a beginning, a middle part, and an end.

3.2.7. 寫作（写作）

A. The School Year Book Committee suggests that seniors write a paragraph to share their most memorable experience in the clubs that they have participated in during their high school years. Write a paragraph to share your experience.

B. As a twelfth-grader, you are invited to write a short article in the school newspaper for the ninth-graders who just entered your high school. In the article, you should highlight your experiences over the past three years and give suggestions as to how to make the best of one's years in high school.

第四課　　職業與愛好
第四課　　职业与爱好

4.1. 各行各業（各行各业）

4.1.1. 生詞練習 （生词练习）

A. 各行各業（各行各业）： Each of the following lines (**a** to **g**) states a situation. From the list, choose the professional whom you would visit in each of the given situations.

律師，記者，建築師，藝術家，醫生，導遊，工程師
律师，记者，建筑师，艺术家，医生，导游，工程师

a. 身體不舒服 （身体不舒服） ＿＿＿＿＿＿

b. 到外國旅行（到外国旅行） ＿＿＿＿＿＿

c. 想買一幅畫（想买一幅画） ＿＿＿＿＿＿

d. 發表新聞（发表新闻） ＿＿＿＿＿＿

e. 蓋新房子（盖新房子） ＿＿＿＿＿＿

f. 建造道路（建造道路） ＿＿＿＿＿＿

g. 發生法律上的問題（发生法律上的问题） ＿＿＿＿＿＿

B. 填空: Dan and Lisa are thinking about their futures. Fill in appropriate words to complete the paragraph.

Dan's Reflection

責任 ，研究，擔心，穩定，平靜，將來 ，決定
责任 ，研究， 担心， 稳定， 平静， 将来， 决定

　　最近這幾天我每天晚上都睡不著覺。眼看快要畢業了，還不知道＿＿＿＿＿＿要做什麼。我找老師＿＿＿＿＿＿這個問題,老師要我別＿＿＿＿＿＿，他說只要盡自己目前當學生的＿＿＿＿＿＿， ＿＿＿＿＿＿一定能找到一個＿＿＿＿＿＿的工作。 現在我心裡＿＿＿＿＿＿多了。

★ ★ ★ ★ ★

　　最近这几天我每天晚上都睡不着觉。眼看快要毕业了，还不知道＿＿＿＿＿＿要做什么。 我找老师＿＿＿＿＿＿这个问题,老师要我别＿＿＿＿＿＿， 他说只要尽自己目前当学生的＿＿＿＿＿＿， ＿＿＿＿＿＿一定能找到一个＿＿＿＿＿＿的工作。 现在我心里＿＿＿＿＿＿多了。

Lisa's Reflection

醫藥 ，書法 ，有關 ，志同道合， 負責 医药，书法，有关，志同道合， 负责

　　我學中文已經三年了，對中文的興趣越來越高，尤其是傳統＿＿＿＿＿＿，我常常廢寢忘食地練習毛筆字。父母老師都說我是個細心內向的人，對工作非常＿＿＿＿＿＿，將來應該做跟傳統＿＿＿＿＿＿的研究，這方面對美國人的健康也許會大有幫助。 我個人也打算利用在中國的時候學學武術，我有信心能找到＿＿＿＿＿＿的朋友一起學武術！

★ ★ ★ ★ ★

　　我学中文已经三年了，对中文的兴趣越来越高，尤其是传统＿＿＿＿＿＿，我常常废寝忘食地练习毛笔字。父母老师都说我是个细心内向的人，对工作非常＿＿＿＿＿＿，将来应该做跟传统＿＿＿＿＿＿的研究，这方面对美国人的健康也许会大有帮助。 我个人也打算利用在中国的时候学学武术，我有信心能找到＿＿＿＿＿＿的朋友一起学武术！

4.1.2. 聽力（听力）: Listen to the conversations and complete the rejoinders. You will hear two short conversations or parts of conversations followed by four choices, designated (A), (B), (C), and (D). Choose the one that continues or completes the conversation in a logical and culturally appropriate manner.

1. (　　)　　2. (　　)

4.1.3. 短文閱讀（短文阅读）: Daming wrote about his hobby and profession. Select the correct answers for the following multiple-choice questions, based on his statements.

大明的愛好

我對數學特別有興趣，從小就愛有數字的東西，可以一個人研究數學問題到廢寢忘食的地步。我父母老是向別人說我是數學小天才，其實我覺得數學是所有科目當中最簡單的，要是碰到一道難題，只要靜心研究就一定能解決。我打算將來從事跟數學有關的職業，到大學當數學教授、做研究。不過我得努力學習，先得到博士學位再說吧。

★ ★ ★ ★ ★

大明的爱好

我对数学特别有兴趣，从小就爱有数字的东西，可以一个人研究数学问题到废寝忘食的地步。我父母老是向别人说我是数学小天才，其实我觉得数学是所有科目当中最简单的，要是碰到一道难题，只要静心研究就一定能解决。我打算将来从事跟数学有关的职业，到大学当数学教授、做研究。不过我得努力学习，先得到博士学位再说吧。

---

1. What does Daming like?
    a) Language   b) Math   c) Biology

2. How do his parents refer to him?
    a) a genius   b) a spoiled kid   c) a nerd

3. What does he want to be in the future?
    a) a scientist   b) a finance analyst   c) a teacher

4. What degree should he get to fulfill his goal?
    a) B.A.   b) M.A.   c) Ph.D.

4.1.4. 口語回答（口语回答）: For the speech sample, you will need to answer five questions. After you hear each question, you will have twenty seconds to record your response. For each question, you should respond as fully and as appropriately as possible.

4.1.5. 課堂口語活動（课堂口语活动）

A. 看圖說話（看图说话）

麗莎的愛好（丽莎的爱好）: Describe Lisa's interests based on the drawings.

B. 美國高中生的愛好（美国高中生的爱好）: You are currently studying abroad in Tianjin. You are asked by your Chinese friends about hobbies common among American high school students. From your perspective, give a short speech describing several representative hobbies that high school students in the United States enjoy and explain why those hobbies are popular.

4.1.6. 寫作（写作）

A. You are a transfer student in 長春 57 中學（长春 57 中学）. You are invited by the school newspaper to write about yourself. Write a paragraph describing yourself, including your hobbies and future plans. Describe how you became interested in these hobbies in the first place. What impact have they had on you? How do you think of expanding them in the future? Use the words in the box.

> 喜歡，擅長，希望，研究，經驗，興趣，當，決定
> 喜欢，擅长，希望，研究，经验，兴趣，当，决定

B. Choose a famous person who is an expert or a professional in a certain area, such as Jackie Chan, Mark Twain, Bill Gates, Jane Goodall, or the like. Write about the person's process and experience of building his or her career based on your research. Also, include what you have learned from that person's experience.

4.2. 選擇職業（选择职业）

4.2.1. 生詞練習（生词练习）

A. 解釋生詞（解释生词）: **a** to **h** are explanations for the words in the box. Find the appropriate one for each word.

> 選擇，結婚，放棄，解決，從事，買得起，到處
> 选择，结婚，放弃，解决，从事，买得起，到处

a. _____ 不再做一件事情

b. _____ 替一個問題找到答案或處理的方法
（替一个问题找到答案或处理的方法）

c. _____ 有錢，可以買東西（有钱，可以买东西）

d. _____ 在不同的事情中，決定要做哪一件

e. _____ 做一件工作或一個職業（做一件工作或一个职业）

f. _____ 每個地方（每个地方）

g. _____ 兩個人成為先生太太（两个人成为先生太太）

B. 填空: Wensheng is talking about his future plans. Fill in the appropriate words from the list to complete the following paragraph.

> 責任，穩定，從事，選擇，擔心，研究，結婚，職業，社會，導遊
>
> ### 文生的未來
>
> 我從小就對旅行有興趣，最喜歡跟父母到各地去看看外國人的生活情形，_____那個_____的特點。就因為如此，我將來想_____的_____是_____。我的_____是要向遊客介紹當地的風土人情和文化特色。父母對我這樣的_____有一點兒_____。他們說這種工作不太_____，畢業以後做做也許還可以，可是_____以後有了家，恐怕就不那麼方便了。

责任，稳定，从事，选择，担心，研究，结婚，职业，社会，导游

　　我从小就对旅行有兴趣，最喜欢跟父母到各地去看看外国人的生活情形，＿＿＿＿＿那个＿＿＿＿＿的特点。就因为如此，我将来想＿＿＿＿＿的＿＿＿＿＿是＿＿＿＿＿。我的＿＿＿＿＿是要向遊客介绍当地的风土人情和文化特色。父母对我这样的＿＿＿＿＿有一点儿＿＿＿＿＿。他们说这种工作不太＿＿＿＿＿，毕业以后做做也许还可以，可是＿＿＿＿＿以后有了家，恐怕就不那么方便了。

C. 填空: Chen Jing is contemplating her career plans for the next ten years.

放棄，提高，政治，至於，未來，學位，解決
放弃，提高，政治，至于，未来，学位，解决

　　最近我常思考的問題就是大學畢業以後到底該做什麼。我對＿＿＿＿＿很有興趣，可是該從事什麼職業呢？雖然現在想還太早，但是我想早點為＿＿＿＿＿打算，早點＿＿＿＿＿一些問題。我希望能得到更高的＿＿＿＿＿，碩士也許能＿＿＿＿＿找到好工作的機會，＿＿＿＿＿博士學位，我也不會＿＿＿＿＿這個可能性。要是能半工半讀，同時兼顧工作和學位，那就是最理想的了。

★ ★ ★ ★ ★

　　最近我常思考的问题就是大学毕业以后到底该做什么，我对＿＿＿＿＿很有兴趣，可是该从事什么职业呢？虽然现在想还太早，但是我想早点为＿＿＿＿＿打算，早点＿＿＿＿＿一些问题，我希望能得到更高的＿＿＿＿＿，硕士也许能＿＿＿＿＿找到好工作的机会，＿＿＿＿＿博士学位，我也不会＿＿＿＿＿这个可能性，要是能半工半读，同时兼顾工作和学位，那就是最理想的了。

4.2.2. 聽力（听力）

A. Teacher Zhang, a counselor at a Taipei High School, has been invited to a radio station to give advice to high school students regarding planning one's career. Listen to Teacher Zhang's advice. Based on what you hear, check the box if the statement is true.

Teacher Zhang…

a. ❑ said that students had to consider a profession's expected income.

b. ❑ advised students to exercise regularly if they land a good job.

c. ❑ asked students to reflect on three questions and said that one positive answer will suffice.

d. ❑ thinks all trades and professions require higher degrees.

e. ❑ believes that neither love for cooking nor business requires future improvement.

f. ❑ thinks there is a need for every profession in the future society.

B. You will hear two short conversations, in which Teacher Zhang is counseling two students, followed by four choices, designated (A), (B), (C), and (D). Choose the one that continues or completes the conversation in a logical and culturally appropriate manner.

　　　　1. (　　) 　2. (　　)

4.2.3. 短文閱讀（短文阅读）：Fang Dawu, a Chinese high school student, is writing an e-mail to his pen pal, Jack, at Mountview High School. Answer the following questions based on the e-mail.

傑克，

高考快到了，今年我完全沒有輕鬆的時候，每天除了考試還是考試。父母和老師都為我們擔心，我倒是很平靜，反正考得好，明年就上大學，考不好，就再準備一年。為了高考，我已經每天都廢寢忘食了，他們還能要我做什麼呢？我真不明白，一次考試就能決定我的未來，你說這公平嗎？你的選擇就比我的多多了，我真希望能像你們美國一樣。你在學校時不但能兼顧學習和個人的愛好，畢業以後還能自己決定想從事什麼樣的職業，要是中國的教育也能跟美國的一樣有彈性，那該多好啊！

不能再寫了，還得準備明天的考試呢。再談！

大武

★★★★★

杰克，

高考快到了，今年我完全没有轻松的时候，每天除了考试还是考试。父母和老师都为我们担心，我倒是很平静，反正考得好，明年就上大学，考不好，就再准备一年。为了高考，我已经每天都废寝忘食了，他们还能要我做什么呢？我真不明白，一次考试就能决定我的未来，你说这公平吗？你的选择就比我的多多了，我真希望能像你们美国一样。你在学校时不但能兼顾学习和个人的爱好，毕业以后还能自己决定想从事什么样的职业，要是中国的教育也能跟美国的一样有弹性，那该多好啊！

不能再写了，还得准备明天的考试呢。再谈！

大武

回答問題（回答问题）：

a. 大武在準備什麼大事？
大武在准备什么大事？

b. 大武覺得怎麼樣？為什麼？
大武觉得怎么样？为什么？

c. 大武的父母和老師覺得怎麼樣？為什麼？
大武的父母和老师觉得怎么样？为什么？

d. 大武說中國的教育和美國的有什麼不同？你同意嗎？
大武说中国的教育和美国的有什么不同？你同意吗？

4.2.4. 實文閱讀（实文阅读）： This is a résumé form for applying for a summer job. You are interested in the job. Read and fill out the form.

履歷表（履历表）		
姓名	姓名	
性別	性别	
出生日期	出生日期	
學校	学校	
電話	电话	
電郵地址	电邮地址	
地址	地址	
教育程度	教育程度	
專業	专业	
主修課程	主修课程	
選修課	选修课	
個人能力	个人能力	
語言能力	语言能力	
其他技能	其他技能	
工作經歷	工作经历	
業餘愛好	业余爱好	

4.2.5. 課堂口語報告（课堂口语报告）

A. Divide the class into two teams and debate the pros and cons of pursuing a job that one does not enjoy, but that makes a lot of money

B. You have already talked about where you see yourself in ten years. Now imagine yourself in twenty years. Give a short report describing what you would be doing at that time. Do you have a clear picture in mind of what you will be like in twenty years?

4.2.6. 看圖寫作（看图写作）： The four pictures tell a story. Imagine that you are writing the story to a friend. Narrate a complete story as suggested by the pictures. Give your story a beginning, a middle part, and an end.

4.2.7. 寫作 （写作）

A. In the reading of 4.2.1 in the textbook, Li Ming wrote an e-mail to Wensheng, saying that he has to make a decision regarding his future career in his senior year in school. Write an e-mail on behalf of Wensheng, stating your thoughts about making a career decision in high school. For example, do you think you can make that decision? What are the pros and cons of making that decision so early?

B. To help senior high school students plan for their future careers, your class decides to compile a booklet of career information. Each of you chooses a career and does research with respect to that job's responsibilities, requirements, pay, working environment, etc. Write a paragraph about what you find. The class can work together to compile the booklet.

C. Write an essay on your ideal job. Explain why you chose this job and how you would land such a job. Also, discuss whether the job is connected to your hobbies or meets your family's expectations. Use as much vocabulary from the lesson as possible.

第五課　　運動與制服
第五课　　运动与制服

5.1.1. 生詞練習（生词练习）

A. 奧運會（奧运会）： Please check (√) the sports that are included in the Olympic Games:

a. ❑高爾夫球（高尔夫球）　　　　g. ❑乒乓球

b. ❑籃球（篮球）　　　　　　　　h. ❑足球

c. ❑跳水（跳水）　　　　　　　　i. ❑游泳

d. ❑網球（网球）　　　　　　　　j. ❑滑冰

e. ❑橄欖球（橄榄球）　　　　　　k. ❑棒球

f. ❑排球　　　　　　　　　　　　l. ❑滑雪

B. 完成句子： Complete each of the following sentences to make a coherent statement.

a. 如果你想申請到大學獎學金，＿＿＿＿＿＿＿＿＿＿＿＿＿＿＿＿。

如果你想申请到大学奖学金，＿＿＿＿＿＿＿＿＿＿＿＿＿＿＿＿。

b. 我生活最重要的一部分＿＿＿＿＿＿＿＿＿＿＿＿＿＿＿＿＿＿。

我生活最重要的一部分＿＿＿＿＿＿＿＿＿＿＿＿＿＿＿＿＿＿。

c. 我對＿＿＿＿＿＿＿＿＿＿＿＿＿＿＿＿＿＿＿＿很熱衷。

我对＿＿＿＿＿＿＿＿＿＿＿＿＿＿＿＿＿＿＿＿很热衷。

d. 我父母常常鼓勵我＿＿＿＿＿＿＿＿＿＿＿＿＿＿＿＿＿＿＿。

我父母常常鼓励我＿＿＿＿＿＿＿＿＿＿＿＿＿＿＿＿＿＿＿。

e. 如果在高中想要受歡迎＿＿＿＿＿＿＿＿＿＿＿＿＿＿＿＿＿。

如果在高中想要受欢迎＿＿＿＿＿＿＿＿＿＿＿＿＿＿＿＿＿。

C. 填空: A student is expressing her admiration for Michelle Kwan in the following paragraph. Please fill in appropriate words to complete the paragraph.

金牌，加油，運動員，冠軍，贏得，世界
金牌，加油，运动员，冠军，赢得，世界

關穎珊是一位出色的滑冰_____。她從小苦練滑冰技巧，十五歲就_____了全美花式滑冰的_____。她還得過五次_____花樣滑冰的_____，在奧運比賽中也得過銀牌和銅牌。我常常去看她的比賽，為她_____。

★ ★ ★ ★ ★

关颖珊是一位出色的滑冰_____。她从小苦练滑冰技巧，十五岁就_____了全美花式滑冰的_____。她还得过五次_____花样滑冰的_____，在奥运比赛中也得过银牌和铜牌。我常常去看她的比赛，为她_____。

5.1.2. 聽力（听力）: Listen to the phone conversations and complete the rejoinders. You will hear two short conversations or parts of conversations followed by four choices, designated (A), (B), (C), and (D). Choose the one that continues or completes the conversation in a logical and culturally appropriate manner.

1. (　　) 2. (　　　)

5.1.3 短文閱讀（短文阅读）： You will read two short articles on two sport events. After reading the articles, please fill out the following chart in English.

參加馬拉松比賽

　　今年春季，李老師參加了波士頓一年一次的馬拉松長跑比賽。參加比賽的運動員是來自世界各地的長跑愛好者。長跑的距離二十六英里，要一口氣跑完。李老師對長跑運動非常熱衷，雖然他不是運動健將，但是他的比賽精神和運動健將是一樣的。馬拉松比賽開始後沒多久，他就跑在大部分運動員的後面了，可是他不灰心，堅持到最後，他是最後一個跑完馬拉松的運動員。先不必說他的長跑成績，大家都被他的精神所感動，為他感到驕傲。

麻省游泳比賽

　　麻薩諸塞州每年十月都會舉行一次全省的游泳比賽。謝琳是大波士頓地區的選手，她去參加了今年的比賽。謝琳從小學就開始接受游泳訓練，她的比賽項目是五百公尺自由式。這次比賽她有點緊張，但是比賽一開始，她就像變成了另一個人，精神抖擻。她游得又快又好看，很受觀眾的歡迎，特別是在最後五十公尺的衝刺，她一下子就游到了最前面，贏得了五百公尺自由式的冠軍，創下一分五十秒的紀錄。

★ ★ ★ ★ ★

参加马拉松比赛

今年春季，李老师参加了波士顿一年一次的马拉松长跑比赛。参加比赛的运动员是来自世界各地的长跑爱好者。长跑的距离二十六英里，要一口气跑完。李老师对长跑运动非常热衷，虽然他不是运动健将，但是他的比赛精神和运动健将是一样的。马拉松比赛开始后没多久，他就跑在大部分运动员的后面了，可是他不灰心，坚持到最后，他是最后一个跑完马拉松的运动员。先不必说他的长跑成绩，大家都被他的精神所感动，为他感到骄傲。

麻省游泳比赛

麻萨诸塞州每年十月都会举行一次全省的游泳比赛。谢琳是大波士顿地区的选手，她去参加了今年的比赛。谢琳从小学就开始接受游泳训练，她的比赛项目是五百公尺自由式。这次比赛她有点紧张，但是比赛一开始，她就像变成了另一个人，精神抖擞。她游得又快又好看，很受观众的欢迎，特别是在最后五十公尺的冲刺，她一下子就游到了最前面，赢得了五百公尺自由式的冠军，创下一分五十秒的纪录。

	names of the athletes	the sports they do	the athletes' character and competitive spirit	competition results
first article				
second article				

5.1.4. 口語回答（口语回答）: For the speech sample, you will need to answer six questions. After you hear each question, you will have twenty seconds to record your response. For each question, you should respond as fully and as appropriately as possible.

5.1.5. 課堂口語活動（课堂口语活动）

A. 看圖説話（看图说话）

田徑接力賽（田径接力赛）：Describe the track and field competition in the drawings.

B. 運動員獎學金（运动员奖学金）：Many universities provide scholarships to students who have achieved excellent sports records, even if the grades of some of these students do not qualify them to enter the universities. Divide the class into two teams and debate the fairness of this kind of practice.

5.1.6. 寫作（写作）

A. Choose an athlete that you admire. Do research on the athlete and write a paragraph about him or her focusing on how he or she has achieved excellence in that sport.

B. In the dialogue in 5.1.5 in the textbook, Mark mentioned that Americans are passionate about engaging in sports and that sometimes unathletic students face pressure to be more athletic. Do you agree with him? Write a paragraph to express your opinion.

C. Your best friend practiced every day for a tennis tournament, in hopes of winning the championship in the school district. Unfortunately, he lost badly in the games. Write a letter to comfort and encourage him.

5.2. 談制服（谈制服）

5.2.1.生詞練習（生词练习）

A. 對制服和便服的看法（对制服和便服的看法）： List at least five words to describe your views on 制服 and 便服，words such as 舒服,單調…etc.

制服	
便服	

B. 反義詞（反义词）： Find an appropriate antonym from the list and fill in the blank for each of the words.

> 輸，進行，熱衷，高興，方便，部分，贊成，單調，時髦，未來
> 输，进行，热衷，高兴，方便，部分，赞成，单调，时髦，未来

a. 反對（反对）　＿＿＿＿＿＿　　　　f. 麻煩　　　　＿＿＿＿＿＿

b. 有趣　　　　＿＿＿＿＿＿　　　　g. 以前　　　　＿＿＿＿＿＿

c. 傷心（伤心）＿＿＿＿＿＿　　　　h. 停止　　　　＿＿＿＿＿＿

d. 土氣（土气）＿＿＿＿＿＿　　　　i. 全部　　　　＿＿＿＿＿＿

e. 贏　　　　　＿＿＿＿＿＿　　　　j. 冷淡　　　　＿＿＿＿＿＿

C. 請舉例（请举例）： Each of the following phrases describes an object, a person, or a matter. Give a concrete example for each description. The answer is provided for **a**.

a. 一雙名牌的球鞋（一双名牌的球鞋）　　　　<u>Nike (耐吉)</u>

b. 一位有名的運動員（一位有名的运动员）　　　　＿＿＿＿＿＿

c. 不對的行為（不对的行为）　　　　＿＿＿＿＿＿

d. 一件不公平的事情（一件不公平的事情）　　　　＿＿＿＿＿＿

e. 一條學校的規定（一条学校的规定）　　　　＿＿＿＿＿＿

D. 填空: Su Ming is a popular athlete at his school. The following paragraph explains his popularity. Fill in an appropriate word from the list to complete the following paragraph.

鼓勵，代表，行為，表現，受歡迎
鼓励，代表，行为，表现，受欢迎

　　蘇明是我們排球隊的隊長，是學校最_____的運動員。他的球技極佳，每次比賽的_____都很突出。他個性開朗、做人謙虛，比賽的時候總是不斷_____隊員。他也常常提醒我們球員：「我們出去比賽是_____學校，一定要注意自己的_____，盡全力打球為學校爭光！」

★★★★★

　　苏明是我们排球队的队长，是学校最_____的运动员。他的球技极佳，每次比赛的_____都很突出。他个性开朗、做人谦虚，比赛的时候总是不断_____队员。他也常常提醒我们球员："我们出去比赛是_____学校，一定要注意自己的_____，尽全力打球为学校争光！"

5.2.2. 聽力（听力）

A. You will hear a phone message left by Da Li for Lan Lan. He wants Lan Lan to inform other students of the contents of this message via e-mail. Listen to the phone message and write an e-mail to relay the message to other students.

Write the e-mail in Chinese for Tiantian and Li Chao.

B. Listen to the conversations and complete the rejoinders. You will hear two short conversations or parts of conversations followed by four choices, designated (A), (B), (C), and (D). Choose the one that continues or completes the conversation in a logical and culturally appropriate manner.

1. (   ) 2. (   )

5.2.3. 短文閱讀（短文阅读）： Xiaofang spent a weekend watching her cousin in the Boston Special Olympics. She sent Da Ming an e-mail after she went home. Based on the e-mail, provide the answers in Chinese for the following three questions.

表哥：

我很高興去波士頓看了你的特殊奧林匹克比賽，為你加油。你和你的朋友們雖然不是運動健將，不是田徑場上的運動明星，但是你們的比賽精神和運動健將、運動明星們是一樣的。你和你的三位接力隊友，互相鼓勵、互相幫助，跑完了接力賽的全程。你們有運動員的風格和勇氣，我真為你們感到驕傲。我想告訴你，上個星期我度過了一個非常有意義的週末。明年你的特殊奧林匹克比賽，我一定還會來為你加油。

小芳

★ ★ ★ ★ ★

表哥：

我很高兴去波士顿看了你的特殊奥林匹克比赛，为你加油。你和你的朋友们虽然不是运动健将，不是田径场上的运动明星，但是你们的比赛精神和运动健将、运动明星们是一样的。你和你的三位接力队友，互相鼓励、互相帮助，跑完了接力赛的全程。你们有运动员的风格和勇气，我真为你们感到骄傲。我想告诉你，上个星期我度过了一个非常有意义的周末。明年你的特殊奥林匹克比赛，我一定还会来为你加油。

小芳

---

a. 小芳上個週末做什麼？
   小芳上个周末做什么？

b. 小芳的表哥參加了什麼運動比賽？
   小芳的表哥参加了什么运动比赛？

c. 小芳的表哥和他的朋友在比賽時表現得怎麼樣？請說明。
   小芳的表哥和他的朋友在比赛时表现得怎么样？请说明。

5.2.4. 實文閱讀（实文阅读）: Answer the following questions in English based on the authentic reading.

校服設計比賽

銘心高中明年將實行穿校服的規定。現在我們正在徵求同學們關於校服的顏色和款式的意見，希望有興趣設計校服的同學們踴躍參加。參加者須交冬夏校服兩份設計圖。設計圖樣請於十一月三日之前交到辦公樓 301 號房。十二月中學校將選出最佳的設計圖並贈與設計者獎金五百元。

負責人：美術老師, 李楠
電子郵件：nli@mingxinhigh.tx.us

校服设计比赛

铭心高中明年将实行穿校服的规定。现在我们正在征求同学们关于校服的颜色和款式的意见，希望有兴趣设计校服的同学们踊跃参加。参加者须交冬夏校服两份设计图。设计图样请于十一月三日之前交到办公楼 301 号房。十二月中学校将选出最佳的设计图并赠与设计者奖金五百元。

负责人：美术老师, 李楠
电子邮件：nli@mingxinhigh.tx.us

---

a. What is the competition about?

b. What do the students need to do if they are interested in it?

c. Who is in charge of the project?

d. What will happen to the winner?

5.2.5. 課堂口語活動（课堂口语活动）

A. Uniform Design: Students are divided into small groups and each group picks a sports team. The task is to design uniforms for the teams. Each group presents to the class the designs for their uniforms and explains why the colors and patterns were chosen.

B. Divide the class into two groups and debate the following issue: Should high school students wear uniforms?

5.2.6. 看圖寫作（看图写作）

The four pictures tell a story. Imagine you are writing the story to a friend. Narrate a complete story as suggested by the pictures. Give your story a beginning, a middle part, and an end.

5.2.7. 寫作 （写作）

A. In the readings and dialogues in lesson 5, some students mentioned "peer pressure" in high schools, such as that regarding wearing fashionable clothing and participating in sports. Are there any other kinds of peer pressure? What are they? How do you face those pressures? Write a short article to express your views and experiences.

B. Your school is soliciting students' opinions regarding whether students should wear uniforms. Write a note to the principal to convince him or her about your views.

第六課　　申請大學和社區服務
第六课　　申请大学和社区服务

6.1.1. 生詞練習（生词练习）

A. 連連看（连连看）： Match the vocabulary with the description.

a.私立　　　　　　　　城市周邊的地區（城市周边的地区）

b.耐心　　　　　　　　付給學校上課的錢（付给学校上课的钱）

c.辦法（办法）　　　　一個地方四周的情況（一个地方四周的情况）

d.學費（学费）　　　　個人辦的學校或公司（个人办的学校或公司）

e.貸款（贷款）　　　　不急，一步步慢慢來（不急，一步步慢慢来）

f.郊區（郊区）　　　　到一個地方去看一看（到一个地方去看一看）

g.環境（环境）　　　　解決問題的方式（解决问题的方式）

h.參觀（参观）　　　　向銀行借來的錢（向银行借来的钱）

B. 反義字（反义字）： Choose an antonym from the list for each the following words. Write the antonym on the blank line.

> 獨立，豐富，優點，寧靜，低，離開，本州，容易，確定，之前
> 独立，丰富，优点，宁静，低，离开，本州，容易，确定，之前

a.困難（困难）＿＿＿＿＿＿＿　　f.未定　　　　　＿＿＿＿＿＿＿

b.不夠　　　　＿＿＿＿＿＿＿　　g.喧嘩（喧哗）＿＿＿＿＿＿＿

c.以後（以后）＿＿＿＿＿＿＿　　h.高　　　　　　＿＿＿＿＿＿＿

d.回來（回来）＿＿＿＿＿＿＿　　i.缺點（缺点）＿＿＿＿＿＿＿

e.外州　　　　＿＿＿＿＿＿＿　　j.依賴（依赖）＿＿＿＿＿＿＿

C. 簡答題（简答题）： Briefly answer the following questions.

a. 推薦信的內容通常包括什麼？
   推荐信的内容通常包括什么？

b. 你對你的高中成績滿意嗎？為什麼？
   你对你的高中成绩满意吗？为什么？

c. 根據就業的情況，現在容易找到工作嗎？
   根据就业的情况，现在容易找到工作吗？

d. 根據你自己的愛好，什麼職業最適合你？
   根据你自己的爱好，什么职业最适合你？

e. 你對什麼樣的文藝活動有興趣？
   你对什么样的文艺活动有兴趣？

f. 你參觀過幾所大學？你對哪一所大學印象特別好？為什麼？
   你参观过几所大学？你对哪一所大学印象特别好？为什么？

g. 通常你自己定的目標是否都達到了？舉一個例子。
   通常你自己定的目标是否都达到了？举一个例子。

h. 你比較喜歡住在城市還是郊區？為什麼？
   你比较喜欢住在城市还是郊区？为什么？

D. 申請大學（申请大学）: Your counselor is helping you keep track of the steps for applying to college and gives you the form below. Unfortunately, you were in a hurry and carelessly stuck it in your jacket pocket, where it went through the laundry. You still have the note but some words are not legible anymore. Figure out the missing words and check off the steps you've already taken:

同學們，請注意！現在快到了一月份，你是否已經⋯

❑ 想過哪一種類型的學校最⋯你
❑ ⋯不同的學校
❑ 請老師寫⋯
❑ ⋯寫申請表
❑ 申請⋯貸款

同学们，请注意！现在快到了一月份，你是否已经⋯

❑ 想过哪一种类型的学校最⋯你
❑ ⋯不同的学校
❑ 请老师写⋯
❑ ⋯写申请表
❑ 申请⋯贷款

6.1.2. 聽力（听力）: Listen to the conversations and complete the rejoinders. You will hear two short conversations or parts of conversations followed by four choices, designated (A), (B), (C), and (D). Choose the one that continues or completes the conversation in a logical and culturally appropriate manner.

1. (　　) 2. (　　)

6.1.3. 短文閱讀（短文阅读）： Xiao Ying wrote the letter below to an old college classmate, Wang Lili, describing her first year after graduation. After reading her letter, answer the questions below.

給王麗麗的信

麗麗：

　　你好！好久沒有跟你聯絡了，你好嗎？

　　不知道你是否還記得畢業那天你跟我說的一句話？我可沒有忘記，而且印象很深刻。你跟我說：「你選的這個科系，就業機會不多，但是我知道你的目標不在於賺錢而是讓自己有豐富多彩的生活。千萬別放棄你的目標！」

　　因為我父母一直對我從事藝術工作不滿意，所以那天你說的那句話真的給了我很大的鼓勵。那時我一方面擔心找不到工作，沒辦法早點還清大學貸款，同時又想獨立生活，不要造成父母的負擔。這一年我的壓力真不小。我先是在媽媽的公司工作了半年，但是大城市生活費高，環境喧嘩，晚上和週末根本沒心情畫畫，所以最後決定到鄉下去住，教小朋友畫畫。雖然是鄉下，但是其實有很多藝術家，藝文活動不少，生活費也低，所以生活還過得去，而且有很多時間畫畫兒。我申請就讀美術學院，上個星期收到了芝加哥藝術學院的通知書，明年不但可以入學，而且有相當多的獎學金，應該不必再貸款，連我父母都為我高興了。我終於可以鬆一口氣了！

　　有空希望你能給我寫信，告訴我你的近況以及將來的計畫等等。很想你！！

　　　　　　　　　　祝

平安

　　　　　　　　　　　　　　小英　上

　　　　　　　　　　　　　　十月五日

给王丽丽的信

丽丽：

你好！好久没有跟你联络了，你好吗？

不知道你是否还记得毕业那天你跟我说的一句话？我可没有忘记，而且印象很深刻。你跟我说：「你选的这个科系，就业机会不多，但是我知道你的目标不在于赚钱而是让自己有丰富多彩的生活。千万别放弃你的目标！」

因为我父母一直对我从事艺术工作不满意，所以那天你说的那句话真的给了我很大的鼓励。那时我一方面担心找不到工作，没办法早点还清大学贷款，同时又想独立生活，不要造成父母的负担。这一年我的压力真不小。我先是在妈妈的公司工作了半年，但是大城市生活费高，环境喧哗，晚上和周末根本没心情画画，所以最后决定到乡下去住，教小朋友画画。虽然是乡下，但是其实有很多艺术家，艺文活动不少，生活费也低，所以生活还过得去，而且有很多时间画画儿。我申请就读美术学院，上个星期收到了芝加哥艺术学院的通知书，明年不但可以入学，而且有相当多的奖学金，应该不必再贷款，连我父母都为我高兴了。我终于可以松一口气了！

有空希望你能给我写信，告诉我你的近况以及将来的计划等等。很想你！！

祝

平安

小英　上

十月五日

a. What did Xiaoying worry about upon graduation?
1) She could not get into an art institute.
2) She could not get used to life in the city.
3) She could not support herself.
4) She could not get financial support from her parents.

b. What did Wang Lili say to her at the graduation ceremony?
   1) She urged Xiao Ying to find a job.
   2) She encouraged Xiao Ying to pursue her dream.
   3) She suggested that Xiao Ying apply for graduate school.
   4) She recommended that Xiao Ying live in the countryside.

c. What did Xiao Ying do right after graduation?
   1) She worked for her mother.
   2) She found a teaching job.
   3) She painted only on weekends.
   4) She enjoyed living in the city.

d. What happened to Xiao Ying recently?
   1) She has been able to devote herself to painting without working.
   2) She has met many artists in the city.
   3) Her parents are willing to provide her financial support.
   4) She has received a scholarship.

6.1.4. 口語回答（口语回答）：For the speech sample, you will need to answer six questions. After you hear each question, you have twenty seconds to record your response. For each question, you should respond as fully and appropriately as possible.

6.1.5. 課堂口語活動（课堂口语活动）

A. 秦林申請大學（秦林申请大学）：Describe the process of Qin Lin's application for colleges based on the drawings.

B. Role-Play Activity: Work with a partner to role-play on the subject of choosing and applying to colleges. Imagine that one of you is a counselor at your school, and work to draw out your partner, the student. The counselor and the student will discuss factors such as proximity to home, costs, environment, grades, SAT results, possible majors, etc., and the various steps in the application process. Based on their discussion, the counselor suggests the various kinds of colleges that are suitable for the student to apply to.

6.1.6. 寫作（写作）

A. You've probably been thinking about the college application process for some time. What advice have you gotten from your parents, counselor, teachers, friends, and older siblings? Choose at least three people in your life with whom you've discussed the topic, and describe what their advice was, how it has or hasn't influenced your decision-making process, and why. Use the words in the following box in your writing.

> 包括，是否，情況，根據，是...可是...，確定
> 包括，是否，情况，根据，是...可是...，确定

B. You've learned about the college entrance examination in Taiwan and China, which is very different from the college entrance process in the United States. Which system do you prefer, or if you don't completely favor one over the other, what are the relative advantages and disadvantages of each? Write a paragraph to answer these questions, giving examples.

6.2. 社區服務（社区服务）

6.2.1 生詞練習（生词练习）

A. 連連看（连连看）： Match the vocabulary with the description.

a.願望（愿望）　　　　課外幫助學生學習（课外帮助学生学习）

b.報告（报告）　　　　村莊裏（村庄里）

c.關心（关心）　　　　保持一樣，不改變（保持一样，不改变）

d.責任（责任）　　　　把事情正式告訴別人（把事情正式告诉别人）

e.將來（将来）　　　　常放在心上

f.一直（一直）　　　　應該做的事情（应该做的事情）

g.輔導（辅导）　　　　以後的時間（以后的时间）

h.鄉下（乡下）　　　　希望能達到的目標（希望能达成的目标）

B. 填空： The following paragraph was written by a high school student exploring volunteer opportunities.　Fill in the blanks with the vocabulary listed at the top.

結束，服務，願望，一直，知識，相信，義工，了解，改變

　　　　學校的學生顧問鼓勵我夏天找個社區＿＿＿＿＿＿機會，不但可以一邊學習新＿＿＿＿＿＿，一邊得到校外的經驗。而且對我將來決定大學專業可能會有很大的幫助。所以這幾個月我都在找尋當＿＿＿＿＿的機會。

　　　　我從小＿＿＿＿＿＿有一個＿＿＿＿＿＿，就是當一個環境科學家。所以當我聽到附近的國家公園需要義工時，興奮極了！這份工作有點辛苦，每天從早上到晚上都在外面跑，但是我＿＿＿＿＿＿我會喜歡的。這個工作一定可以讓我更＿＿＿＿＿環境科學，也可以認識國家公園裏的科學家，說不定這個經驗會＿＿＿＿＿＿我的一生。

　　　　我上個星期已經填好並且寄出了申請表，這兩個星期之內應該會收到通知。現在真希望這個學年快點＿＿＿＿＿＿，好讓我在暑假有一些不同的經驗！

結束，服務，願望，一直，知識，相信，義工，了解，改變

　　　学校的学生顾问鼓励我夏天找个社区_____机会，不但可以一边学习新_____，一边得到校外的经验。而且对我将来决定大学专业可能会有很大的帮助。所以这几个月我都在找寻当_____的机会。

　　　我从小_____有一个_____，就是当一个环境科学家。所以当我听到附近的国家公园需要义工时，兴奋极了！这份工作有点辛苦，每天从早上到晚上都在外面跑，但是我_____我会喜欢的。这个工作一定可以让我更_____环境科学，也可以认识国家公园里的科学家，说不定这个经验会_____我的一生。

　　　我上个星期已经填好并且寄出了申请表，这两个星期之内应该会收到通知。现在真希望这个学年快点_____，好让我在暑假有一些不同的经验！

6.2.2. 聽力（听力）

A. You will hear a report given by Wang Xiaolan regarding her community service last semester. Your friend Jian Xiong is very interested in doing a similar volunteer job, but he is unable to come to school today. He asked you to jot down the main information from Wang Xiaolan's report. Listen to the recording and then write down the main information from her report for Jian Xiong.

B. Listen to the conversations and complete the rejoinders. You will hear two short conversations or parts of conversations followed by four choices, designated (A), (B), (C), and (D). Choose the one that continues or completes the conversation in a logical and culturally appropriate manner.

1. (　　) 2. (　　)

6.2.3. 閱讀、寫作（阅读、写作）： Li Xiaoliang has written an e-mail to get your advice. Read the e-mail she sent and write an e-mail to respond to her questions.

嗨：

你好！你有沒有社區服務的經驗？或者聽過別的同學談他們的經驗？不知道社區服務會有什麼樣的收穫？你覺得什麼樣的個性適合從事社區服務？我的個性內向，是否適合社區服務的工作？我打算明年暑假找一個當義工的機會或者打工賺點零用錢。你打過工嗎？社區服務和打工賺錢各有什麼優缺點？如果你有社區服務和打工賺錢這兩個機會，你會選擇哪一個？為什麼？對不起，問你這麼多問題。我知道你經驗豐富，謝謝你的幫助！

小亮

嗨：

你好！你有没有社区服务的经验？或者听过别的同学谈他们的经验？不知道社区服务会有什么样的收获？你觉得什么样的个性适合从事社区服务？我的个性内向，是否适合社区服务的工作？我打算明年暑假找一个当义工的机会或者打工赚点零用钱。你打过工吗？社区服务和打工赚钱各有什么优缺点？如果你有社区服务和打工赚钱这两个机会，你会选择哪一个？为什么？对不起，问你这么多问题。我知道你经验丰富，谢谢你的帮助！

小亮

6.2.4. 實文閱讀（实文阅读）：Read the authentic application and program information from a center looking for volunteers and choose the correct answers for the following multiple-choice questions.

義工申請表

姓名		出生日期		性別	身份證號碼
學歷（圈選一個）		國中　高中　大學			
住宅電話			傳真號碼		
行動電話			電子郵件		
專業/特長					
義工經驗					
想當義工的原因					
想參加的工作類型					

青少年、青年志願工作中心

目的

> 鼓勵青少年、青年參與志工服務，運用所學專長，知識技能以及個人特長，提供社區的需求服務。

> 激發青少年、青年的責任感，履行社區公民的義務，增進與社區民眾的相互了解。

志願者的工作類型

高中、大學學生
- 社區營造
- 教育輔導
- 電腦教學

國中、高中、大學學生
- 環境清潔維護
- 老人生活關懷

所需申請文件
- 申請表格
- 學校課外活動組推薦信
- 父母同意書

义工申请表

姓名	出生日期	性别	身份证号码
学历（圈选一个）	国中　高中　大学		
住宅电话		传真号码	
行动电话		电子邮件	
专业/特长			
义工经验			
想当义工的原因			
想参加的工作类型			

青少年、青年志愿工作中心

目的

➤ 鼓励青少年、青年参与志工服务，运用所学专长，知识技能以及个人特长，提供社区的需求服务。

➤ 激发青少年、青年的责任感，履行社区公民的义务，增进与社区民众的相互了解。

志愿者的工作類型

高中、大学学生
- 社區營造
- 教育辅导
- 电脑教学

国中、高中、大学学生
- 環境清潔維護
- 老人生活关怀

所需申请文件

- 申请表格
- 学校课外活动组推荐信
- 父母同意书

a. The purpose of this volunteer center is
   1) to mobilize young people to help the community grow.
   2) to cultivate young people to become responsible community citizens.
   3) to provide young people with extracurricular activities.
   4) to help young people develop the skills to work with a team.

b. What kinds of information do applicants need to provide in the application form? Circle all those that apply.
   1) gender   2) educational level   3) special talents and abilities
   4) e-mail address   5) work experience   6) home address
   7) previous volunteer experience   8) time available
   9) the kind of volunteering that the applicant prefers

c. What kinds of documents are required when applying for volunteer jobs?
   1) Statement of purpose   2) A recommendation letter from a teacher
   3) Health form   4) Parental agreement

d. What kinds of volunteer jobs can seventh graders participate in?
   1) building houses   2) environmental projects
   3) teaching computer skills 4) tutoring students

6.2.5. 課堂口語活動（课堂口语活动）

A. Prepare a short speech about a volunteer opportunity that you know of either through personal experience or other means, encouraging your audience members to join in. What responsibilities are entailed? How would it help them in future? What kind of influence would they leave behind? What fields of knowledge would they learn? Why would it benefit them over finding a job instead?

B. Not only high school students do volunteer work; profile someone you know personally or just know of who has contributed to the world or their locale after high school. Prepare a short speech about this person: what he or she does, his or her motivation, the influence he or she has had on others, challenges he or she has overcome, and how you know of this person.

6.2.6. 看圖寫作（看图写作）：The four pictures tell a story. Imagine you are writing the story to a friend. Narrate the complete story as suggested by the pictures. Give your story a beginning, a middle part, and an end.

6.2.7. 寫作（写作）

A. Do some research on volunteer opportunities related to your Chinese language ability. These could be in your community or farther away, such as in China or Taiwan. Write about why this work would appeal to you, whether in the immediate future or further on in your life. Try to include the vocabulary provided in the box.

> 知識，情況，改變，推薦，包括，適合，目標，相信，優/缺點，
> 願望，獨立，責任心，豐富，印象，影響
>
> 知识，情况，改变，推荐，包括，适合，目标，相信，优/缺点，
> 愿望，独立，责任心，丰富，印象，影响

B. Write a self-introduction letter to the volunteer organization that you found for the writing task above. In the letter, convince the organization that you are a good and qualified candidate for that volunteer position by describing your qualifications, motivations, experience, how it fits into your future plans, and what you hope to gain from the experience.

第七課　　兩代之間
第七课　　兩代之间

7.1. 父母與孩子（父母与孩子）

7.1.1. 生詞練習（生词练习）

A. 連連看（连连看）： Match the vocabulary on the left with the descriptions on the right.

a. 代溝（代沟）　　　　容易接受新的想法
　　　　　　　　　　　容易接受新的想法

b. 嘮叨（唠叨）　　　　互相用言語傷人
　　　　　　　　　　　互相用言语伤人

c. 允許（允许）　　　　興趣
　　　　　　　　　　　兴趣

d. 合理　　　　　　　　吃的、喝的

e. 開明（开明）　　　　可以接受的要求或者規定
　　　　　　　　　　　可以接受的要求或者规定

f. 吵架　　　　　　　　話多，說不停
　　　　　　　　　　　话多，说不停

g. 穿著（穿着）　　　　父母和孩子對同一件事情有不同的看法
　　　　　　　　　　　父母和孩子对同一件事情有不同的看法

h. 喜好　　　　　　　　身上穿的、戴的

i. 飲食（饮食）　　　　讓你去做你想做的事
　　　　　　　　　　　让你去做你想做的事

B. 填空： Read the paragraph in which Bill is complaining about his parents. Fill in appropriate words from the list below to complete the paragraph.

嘮叨，允許，管，開明，年輕人，繁重，其實，搖滾樂，自由

嘮叨，允许，管，开明，年轻人，繁重，其实，摇滚乐，自由

我覺得我爸媽很不 _____。他們不_____我聽_____、穿迷你裙、染頭髮和刺青。_____我已經長大，不是小孩子了，他們不應該還_____我的穿著、愛好、飲食和交朋友。 我希望我爸媽多了解_____的想法，多給我一點 _____。爸爸媽媽，我的課業已經很_____了，請不要再_____了。

★ ★ ★ ★ ★

我觉得我爸妈很不 _____。他们不 _____我听_____、穿迷你裙、染头发和刺青。_____我已经长大，不是小孩子了，他们不应该还_____我的穿着、爱好、饮食和交朋友。 我希望我爸妈多了解_____的想法，多给我一点 _____。爸爸妈妈，我的课业已经很_____了，请不要再_____了。

C. 完成句子: Choose an appropriate word from the list below to complete each of the following paragraphs.

> 争吵，談得來，自由，代溝，合理，繁重
> 争吵，谈得来，自由，代沟，合理，繁重

a. (　　　　) 王中的媽媽老是管他的穿著、喜好和飲食，因此他和媽媽常常…
王中的妈妈老是管他的穿着、喜好和饮食，因此他和妈妈常常…

b. (　　　　) 瑪莉每天都有很多功課，每個星期的考試也很多，她覺得課業很…
玛莉每天都有很多功课，每个星期的考试也很多，她觉得课业很…

c. (　　　　) 李明和他爸爸兩個人都喜歡聽搖滾樂，在這方面李明覺得跟爸爸很…
李明和他爸爸两个人都喜欢听摇滚乐，在这方面李明觉得跟爸爸很…

d. (　　　　) 陳剛的爸媽要他天天在家看書，不可以和朋友出去玩，他覺得爸媽的要求不…
陈刚的爸妈要他天天在家看书，不可以和朋友出去玩，他觉得爸妈的要求不…

e. (　　　　) 小莉的爸媽不允許她和朋友開車去旅行，不允許她穿迷你裙。小莉覺得爸媽跟她有…
小莉的爸妈不允许她和朋友开车去旅行，不允许她穿迷你裙。小莉觉得爸妈跟她有…

7.1.2. 聽力（听力）: Listen to the conversations and complete the rejoinders. You will hear two short conversations or parts of conversations followed by four choices, designated (A), (B), (C), and (D). Choose the one that continues or completes the conversation in a logical and culturally appropriate manner.

1. (　　) 2. (　　)

7.1.3. 短文閱讀（短文阅读）: Pingping writes a letter to her teacher to share her feelings about how her boyfriend's mother treats her. Based on the letter below, answer the following four questions.

萍萍給王老師的信(萍萍给王老师的信)

王老師：

　　您好！我最近交了一個男朋友。他們家三代同堂。爺爺和爸爸媽媽都是小提琴演奏家，我的男朋友跟他們不一樣，他只喜歡搖滾樂而已，所以他常常為了音樂愛好跟父母爭吵。我喜歡搖滾樂，因此我們很談得來，也常常一塊去聽搖滾音樂會。除此之外，我們都染頭髮和刺青。昨天我們在購物中心遇到他媽媽，她看了我的頭髮和迷你裙一眼，沒跟我說話就走了。今天我男朋友對我說昨天他回家以後，她媽媽就嘮叨個不停，說他不應該那麼早就交女朋友，還說我不是一個乖女孩，要他跟我分手。我真的很喜歡我的男朋友，我該怎麼辦呢？

萍萍 敬上

十一月十二日

★★★★★

王老师：

　　您好！我最近交了一个男朋友。他们家三代同堂。爷爷和爸爸妈妈都是小提琴演奏家，我的男朋友跟他们不一样，他只喜欢摇滚乐而已，所以他常常为了音乐爱好跟父母争吵。我喜欢摇滚乐，因此我们很谈得来，也常常一块去听摇滚音乐会。除此之外，我们都染头发和刺青。昨天我们在购物中心遇到他妈妈，她看了我的头发和迷你裙一眼，没跟我说话就走了。今天我男朋友对我说昨天他回家以后，她妈妈就唠叨个不停，说他不应该那么早就交女朋友，还说我不是一个乖女孩，要他跟我分手。我真的很喜欢我的男朋友，我该怎么办呢？

萍萍 敬上

十一月十二日

a. 萍萍男朋友的家庭是怎樣的一個家庭？
　　萍萍男朋友的家庭是怎样的一个家庭？

b. 萍萍跟她男朋友有什麼一樣的地方？
　　萍萍跟她男朋友有什么一样的地方？

c. 萍萍男朋友的媽媽喜歡她嗎？為什麼？
　　萍萍男朋友的妈妈喜欢她吗？为什么？

d. 萍萍男朋友的媽媽為什麼對她兒子嘮叨？
　　萍萍男朋友的妈妈为什么对她儿子唠叨？

7.1.4. 口語回答（口语回答）： For the speech sample, you will need to answer six questions. After you hear each question, you will have twenty seconds to record your response. For each question, you should respond as fully and as appropriately as possible.

7.1.5. 課堂口語活動（课堂口语活动）

看圖說話（看图说话）

A. 偉力的刺青（伟力的刺青）： Describe what has happened to Willy based on the following drawings.

B. According to a recent survey, high school students expect their parents to spend around \$350 on back-to-school supplies (including books, clothing, electronic gear, etc.). Divide the class into two groups: parents' team and children's team. Debate whether \$350 is a necessary and reasonable expense for a high school student's back-to-school supplies.

7.1.6. 寫作（写作）

A. In the following sign a new regulation is announced by the principal of your school. You are a class president. On behalf of your class, write a petition to the principal to convince him or her that this rule is unreasonable.

各位同學請注意：

從這學期開始，同學來學校上課，不可以染頭髮，或身上有刺青。違反這項規定的同學，將有十天不准來學校。並且校長會立刻通知家長。

各位同学请注意：

从这学期开始，同学来学校上课，不可以染头发，或身上有刺青。违反这项规定的同学，将有十天不准来学校。并且校长会立刻通知家长。

B. Is there a "generation gap" between you and your parents?

If yes, write a short essay to explain what kind of gap exists between you and your parents. How is this gap formed? Do you think it is possible to bridge the gap through communication or any other methods?

If no, write a short essay to explain why there is no gap between you and your parents and give examples to demonstrate how you get along with your parents.

7.2. 兩代的溝通（兩代的沟通）

7.2.1. 生詞練習（生词练习）

A. 解釋生詞（解释生词）：a to **g** are definitions for the words on the left.　Choose an appropriate definition for each word.

_____	溝通 沟通	a.	幫助他人 帮助他人
_____	重視 重视	b.	故意跟人不一樣 故意跟人不一样
_____	體諒 体谅	c.	自己的事自己不做，希望別人幫你做 自己的事自己不做，希望别人帮你做
_____	依賴 依赖	d.	聽父母的話，不讓他們擔心 听父母的话，不让他们担心
_____	分擔 分担	e.	理解別人的困難 理解别人的困难
_____	作對 作对	f.	互相說出心中的話，彼此互相了解 互相说出心中的话，彼此互相了解
_____	孝順 孝顺	g.	覺得重要 觉得重要

B. 你跟父母的相處（你跟父母的相处）： Check the descriptions from **a** to **h** that best describe you and your parents.

a. ❑ 花時間跟你溝通
　　花时间跟你沟通

b. ❑ 跟你一起嘗試不同的事物，接受新的挑戰
　　跟你一起尝试不同的事物，接受新的挑战

c. ❑ 每天叫你復習功課
　　每天叫你复习功课

d. ❑ 跟你分享快樂，幫你分擔煩惱
    跟你分享快乐，帮你分担烦恼

e. ❑ 要求你達到他們的期望
    要求你达到他们的期望

f. ❑ 重視你的興趣
    重视你的兴趣

g. ❑ 幫助你了解自己的能力，找到你的自己的方向
    帮助你了解自己的能力，找到你的自己的方向

h. ❑ 要你自己起床，不要依賴父母叫你
    要你自己起床，不要依赖父母叫你

C. 完成句子: Choose an appropriate word from the list to complete each sentence.

挑戰、體諒、相處、煩惱、方向
挑战、体谅、相处、烦恼、方向

a. （　　　　）做父母的如果沒有耐心，不肯多花時間去了解子
            女，子女就不容易跟他們…
            做父母的如果没有耐心，不肯多花时间去了解子
            女，子女就不容易跟他们…

b. （　　　　）做父母的要了解孩子的興趣和才能，幫助孩子找到
            他們的…
            做父母的要了解孩子的兴趣和才能，帮助孩子找到
            他们的…

c. （　　　　）做子女的應該學習獨立，對自己負責，不要讓父母…
            做子女的应该学习独立，对自己负责，不要让父母…

d. （　　　　）青少年要能嘗試不同的事物、接受新的…
            青少年要能尝试不同的事物、接受新的…

e. （　　　　）做子女的對父母的苦心要能…
            做子女的对父母的苦心要能…

7.2.2. 聽力（听力）

A. Listen to the following conversation. Based on what you hear, select correct answers for the following questions.

a. What bothers the younger sister?
  1) She skipped the violin classes.
  2) Her cell phone was taken away.
  3) Her brother is not home very often.
  4) She is not allowed to see her boyfriend.

b. The brother
  1) lives in an apartment.
  2) used to fight with his mother.
  3) is giving his sister advice.
  4) was very obedient when he was a high school student.

c. What is the brother's experience with their mom?
  1) He couldn't get along with her at all.
  2) It was useless to communicate with her.
  3) It was better to make his own judgments.
  4) She did accept reasonable explanations.

B. Listen to the conversations and complete the rejoinders. You will hear two short conversations or parts of conversations followed by four choices, designated (A), (B), (C), and (D). Choose the one that continues or completes the conversation in a logical and culturally appropriate manner.

1. (   )   2. (   )

7.2.3. 短文閱讀（短文阅读）: In 7.1.3, Pingping wrote a letter to her teacher. Here is her teacher's response. Based on the letter, answer the following three questions.

王老師給萍萍回信(王老师给萍萍的回信)

萍萍：

　　你好！別難過了！天下父母心，每一個父母都愛子女，都望子成龍，望女成鳳。你男朋友的父母是小提琴家，而你男朋友只喜歡搖滾樂。當子女達不到父母的期望，雙方就常常發生爭吵。做父母的通常也不了解為什麼孩子要去染頭髮和刺青。我認為你的男朋友應該試著跟他父母溝通，讓他父母知道你是個好女孩，功課好又彈了一手好鋼琴，你染頭髮和穿迷你裙只是趕時髦而已。也許他可以安排讓你和他父母見面，讓他們認識真正的你。

王老師 上
十一月十六日

★ ★ ★ ★ ★

萍萍：

　　你好！別难过了！天下父母心，每一个父母都爱子女，都望子成龙，望女成凤。你男朋友的父母是小提琴家，而你男朋友只喜欢摇滚乐。当子女达不到父母的期望，双方就常常发生争吵。做父母的通常也不了解为什么孩子要去染头发和刺青。我认为你的男朋友应该试着跟他父母沟通，让他父母知道你是个好女孩，功课好又弹了一手好钢琴，你染头发和穿迷你裙只是赶时髦而已。也许他可以安排让你和他父母见面，让他们认识真正的你。

王老师 上
十一月十六日

a. What is Pingping's strength?
1) She is a good piano player.
2) She knows about fashion.
3) She is good at communicating with people.

b. In Teacher Wang's view, why do her boyfriend and his parents fight often?
1) The parents do not like Pingping.
2) He did not tell his parents about his bad grades.
3) He does not fulfill his parents' expectations.

c. What was the suggestion to Pingping from Teacher Wang?
1) Talk to her boyfriend's mother directly.
2) Ask her boyfriend to communicate with his parents.
3) Write a letter to her boyfriend's parents.

7.2.4. 課堂口語活動（课堂口语活动）

A. In order to understand what "Generation Gap" means, your class decides to do a survey, especially to find out to what extent the parents' generation knows about the contemporary world of high school. In small groups, brainstorm five or six questions that you can ask those adults, such as
- What is the most popular TV program for high school students?
- What is the current fashion on campus?
- What is the most visited Web site for female students?

Each group will interview five parents and report in class the result of the interviews and the evaluation of how wide or narrow the gap is between your and your parents' generation.

B. The Student Council of your school would like to plan an event called "Bridge the Generation Gap." The goal of the event is to learn from the older generation in your local community. For example, Winston High School invited senior citizens from the neighborhood to share their experiences as to how the area has been growing in the past two decades. One of the activities is to take a walking tour around the neighborhood with the senior citizens as guides. In small groups, plan an event for "Bridge the Generation Gap." Each group will present its plans.

C. Skit performance: In a small group, write a three-minute skit and then perform it. The content of the skit should include at least the following two scenes:
1) A conflict between parents and a teenager occurs.
2) The parents and the kid try to work it out.

7.2.5. 看圖寫作（看图写作）： The four pictures tell a story. Imagine you are writing the story to a friend. Narrate a complete story as suggested by the pictures. Give your story a beginning, a middle part, and an end.

7.2.6. 寫作 （写作）

A. Write a letter to your counselor telling her that the reason you could not take the midterm exam yesterday was because you and your mother had an argument the night before on some issues, such as dating, not working hard enough, or the like. Be creative with the issues that your mother complained about.

B. There is a Chinese essay contest in your school district and the theme is "When I become a parent…." You are interested and submit an essay. In the essay, describe the kind of parent you want to become and how you plan to educate your children. Also explain why the approaches that you suggest are important and necessary.

第八課　　年輕人的網路世界
第八课　　年轻人的网络世界

8.1. 網路活動（网络活动）

8.1.1. 生詞練習（生词练习）

A. 日常活動（日常活動）：The following is a list of activities. Choose the appropriate activities to answer each of the following questions.

看影片	購物	寫網誌	寫簡訊	看新聞	寫部落格
下載音樂	即時通訊	參與討論	上傳影片	玩遊戲	認識朋友
分享照片	聊天	聽音樂	做功課	讀電子郵件	聯絡感情

    a. 哪些是在網路上一個人就可以做的事情？

    b. 哪些是在網路上跟別人一起才能做的事情？

    c. 哪些是人越多越有意思的事情？

****

看影片	购物	写网志	写简讯	看新闻	写部落格
下载音乐	即时通讯	参与讨论	上传影片	玩游戏	认识朋友
分享照片	聊天	听音乐	做功课	读电子邮件	联络感情

    a. 哪些是在网络上一个人就可以做的事情？

    b. 哪些是在网络上跟别人一起才能做的事情？

    c. 哪些是人越多越有意思的事情？

B. 連連看（连连看）：Match the words on the left with the appropriate definitions on the right.

a.即時（即时）　　買東西（买东西）

b.陌生　　　　　　告訴演員怎麼演戲的人（告诉演员怎么演戏的人）

c.至少　　　　　　心理的感覺（心理的感觉）

d.好處（好处）　　最少

e.導演（导演）　　馬上、立刻（马上、立刻）

f.購物（购物）　　好的方面

g.參與（参与）　　加入

h.心情　　　　　　不認識的感覺（不认识的感觉）

8.1.2. 聽力（听力）：Listen to the conversations and complete the rejoinders. You will hear two short conversations or parts of conversations followed by four choices, designated (A), (B), (C), and (D). Choose the one that continues or completes the conversation in a logical and culturally appropriate manner.

1. （　　） 2. （　　）

8.1.3. 短文閱讀（短文阅读）：Meihua and Guohua express their views on using the Internet. Check the correct answers after reading their views.

美華的網路世界

我已經上網成癮了，每天上網的時間不知有多少，好像所有的事情都得在網路上才能解決。比方說交朋友、買東西、學習、做作業、玩遊戲、跟人通信等等。我的生活就是網路的生活。

國華的網路世界

我認為網路只是一種工具。網路雖然很方便，可是有時候也很容易發生事情。我對一些網站提供的訊息抱著謹慎的態度。有時候我上網查一些資料或新聞，可是從來不參與跟陌生人的討論。事實上我對上網聊天一點興趣都沒有。

★ ★ ★ ★ ★

美华的网络世界

我已经上网成瘾了，每天上网的时间不知有多少，好像所有的事情都得在网络上才能解决。比方说交朋友、买东西、学习、做作业、玩游戏、跟人通信等等。我的生活就是网络的生活。

国华的网络世界

我认为网络只是一种工具。网络虽然很方便，可是有时候也很容易发生事情。我对一些网站提供的讯息抱着谨慎的态度。有时候我上网查一些资料或新闻，可是从来不参与跟陌生人的讨论。事实上我对上网聊天一点兴趣都没有。

Who is more likely to do the following things online?

		美華（美华）	國華（国华）
a.	shopping	❑	❑
b.	participating in discussion forum	❑	❑
c.	researching	❑	❑
d.	chatting	❑	❑
e.	reading news	❑	❑
f.	playing games	❑	❑

8.1.4. 口語回答（口语回答）： For the speech sample, you will need to answer five questions. After you hear each question, you will have twenty seconds to record your response. For each question, you should respond as fully and as appropriately as possible.

8.1.5. 課堂口語活動（课堂口语活动）

A. 看圖說話 （看图说话）
張華山天天上網 （张华山天天上网）

B. 最佳網站（最佳网站）： Your school plans to compile a list of informative and fun learning Web sites on various subjects for grades 9 through 12. Please suggest one of your favorite Web sites. Demonstrate the Web site and introduce its desirable features in class.

8.1.6. 寫作（写作）

A. Your future university is planning to develop a Web page to orient new students on campus. The university is soliciting your opinion on necessary information that will be helpful for incoming students. Write a paragraph to suggest the design and information for the Web page.

B. Read the following news excerpt. *Two tenth-grade students were sent home after officials learned that they had posted a videotape on YouTube of their teacher losing his temper. YouTube removed the video at the request of the school. The school since then has banned all electronic devices, including cellphones and digital music players.* Should the students be punished for posting the teacher's episode on YouTube? Is it reasonable for the school to ban all electronic devices? Write an article expressing your reaction to this news, including answering the above two questions.

8.2. 網路的影響（网络的影响）
8.2.1. 生詞練習（生词练习）

A. 近義詞、相反詞？（近义词、相反词？）： Write S or A to designate each of the following pairs as synonyms or antonyms. For example, the pair in **a** are synonyms.

a.	不良	不佳	S
b.	奇怪	不特別	
c.	類似（类似）	一樣（一样）	
d.	提高	減低（减低）	
e.	否則	而且	
f.	陌生	熟識（熟识）	
g.	益處（益处）	好處（好处）	
h.	差別	相同	
i.	談論（谈论）	討論（讨论）	
j.	詳細（详细）	清楚	
k.	退步	進步（进步）	
l.	危險（危险）	安全	

B. 網路活動（网络活动）： List four online activities that you frequently engage in. Write down their pros and cons in Chinese.

網路活動 网络活动	好處 好处	壞處 坏处

C. 填空： Zhenzhen and her father, Mr. Li, express their views on the pros and cons of online activities. For each of the following passages, use the vocabulary words at the top to fill in the blanks.

a. 真真的爸爸李先生

工具，資料，查詢，提高，公開，網癮，擔心，上網，危險，不良
工具，资料，查询，提高，公开，网瘾，担心，上网，危险，不良

　　我向來認為網路是這個時代最好的發明。 有了這個_____，
各種資料都能_____到，做任何事情都能_____效率。 現
在到處都可以_____，的確是很方便。唯一讓我_____的是
很多有了_____的年輕人常常在網上_____自己的個人
_____，要是碰到居心_____的陌生人就一定很容易發生
_____啊！

★★★★★

　　我向来认为网络是这个时代最好的发明。 有了这个_____，
各种资料都能_____到，做任何事情都能_____效率。 现
在到处都可以_____，的确是很方便。唯一让我_____的是
很多有了_____的年轻人常常在网上_____自己的个人
_____，要是碰到居心_____的陌生人就一定很容易发生
_____啊！

b. 真真

提供，話題，謹慎，情況，即時，參與，上網，詳細，愉快，網路
提供，话题，谨慎，情况，即时，参与，上网，详细，愉快，网络

　　我從小是跟電腦一起長大的。＿＿＿＿＿＿是我生活的一部分，沒有＿＿＿＿＿很多事情就做不了，更不能＿＿＿＿＿知道世界各地的＿＿＿＿＿。我常上網＿＿＿＿＿各種＿＿＿＿＿的討論，覺得很＿＿＿＿＿。我瞭解爸爸擔心的事情，所以總是很＿＿＿＿，一定不隨便＿＿＿＿＿我個人的＿＿＿＿＿資料。

★ ★ ★ ★ ★

　　我从小是跟计算机一起长大的。＿＿＿＿＿是我生活的一部分，没有＿＿＿＿＿很多事情就做不了，更不能＿＿＿＿＿知道世界各地的＿＿＿＿＿。我常上网＿＿＿＿＿各种＿＿＿＿＿的讨论，觉得很＿＿＿＿＿。我了解爸爸担心的事情，所以总是很＿＿＿＿，一定不随便＿＿＿＿＿我个人的＿＿＿＿＿资料。

8.2.2. 聽力 (听力)

A. A classmate of yours is giving a short speech regarding the Internet. Your teacher asks everyone to write down the main points of the speech in Chinese.

Write three points mentioned in the speech regarding the Internet.

1.＿＿＿＿＿＿＿＿＿＿＿＿＿＿＿＿＿＿＿＿＿＿＿＿＿＿

2.＿＿＿＿＿＿＿＿＿＿＿＿＿＿＿＿＿＿＿＿＿＿＿＿＿＿

3.＿＿＿＿＿＿＿＿＿＿＿＿＿＿＿＿＿＿＿＿＿＿＿＿＿＿

B. Listen to the conversations and complete the rejoinders. You will hear two short conversations or parts of conversations followed by four choices, designated (A), (B), (C), and (D). Choose the one that continues or completes the conversation in a logical and culturally appropriate manner.

1. ( )   2. ( )

8.2.3. 短文閱讀 （短文阅读）：Wang Desheng wrote an e-mail to Da Wei, his pen pal in the United States. Based on the e-mail message, answer the following questions.

大為：

很高興收到你的來信。很抱歉現在才回信。我現在在一個網咖給你寫信。網咖是中國最便宜的上網選擇。我們家買不起電腦，就算買得起電腦，也無法負擔連接互聯網的費用。網咖雖然方便、便宜，但大部分的網咖環境不太好，不但地方小，而且還有很多人抽煙，有的網咖甚至有不適合青少年的電腦遊戲。很多家長不允許孩子到網咖，但還是有不少學生整天在網咖玩遊戲。我跟爸媽說為了寫報告，我得上網查詢資料，他們才讓我來。美國也有網咖嗎?美國網咖的環境怎麼樣？你常到網咖上網嗎？

德生

★ ★ ★ ★ ★

大为：

很高兴收到你的来信。很抱歉现在才回信。我现在在一个网咖给你写信。网咖是中国最便宜的上网选择。我们家买不起计算机，就算买得起计算机，也无法负担连接互联网的费用。网咖虽然方便、便宜，但大部分的网咖环境不太好，不但地方小，而且还有很多人抽烟，有的网咖甚至有不适合青少年的计算机游戏。很多家长不允许孩子到网咖，但还是有不少学生整天在网咖玩游戏。我跟爸妈说为了写报告，我得上网查询资料，他们才让我来。美国也有网咖吗？美国网咖的环境怎么样？你常到网咖上网吗？

德生

---

a. Why did Wang Desheng write Da Wei's e-mail in an Internet café?
   1) He is playing a game there.
   2) His family does not have a computer.
   3) The computer at his house has no access to the Internet.

b. What is Wang Desheng's comment about Internet cafés in China?
   1) Many cool games are offered to teenagers.
   2) One can stay there the whole night working on the computer.
   3) It is usually smoky.

c. Why did Wang Desheng's parents let him to go to the Internet café?
   1) They know he has to write a letter to Da Wei.
   2) His parents are very open-minded.
   3) Desheng convinced them that he needs to do research online for his paper.

8.2.4. 實文閱讀 (實文閱讀)

廣告網	
1. 徵才求職 公司徵才 個人求職 家教補習	2. 房地租售 賣房子 房屋出租
3. 傢俱買賣 買新品 買二手 賣新品 賣二手	4. 交友聯誼 男找女 女找男 聯誼資訊
5. 電腦相關 買二手 賣二手 維修服務	6. 工商服務 商家廣告 尋找服務
7. 社區活動 藝術文化 教育課程 社團活動	8. 更多>>

广告网	
1. 征才求职 公司征才 个人求职 家教补习	2. 房地租售 卖房子 房屋出租
3. 家具买卖 买新品 买二手 卖新品 卖二手	4. 交友联谊 男找女 女找男 联谊信息
5. 计算机相关 买二手 卖二手 维修服务	6. 工商服务 商家广告 寻找服务
7. 社区活动 艺术文化 教育课程 社团活动	8. 更多>>

Choose an appropriate answer for each question, based on the previous authentic reading.

a. What information is provided?
    1) features of the newest electronic gadgets
    2) constantly updated daily weather reports
    3) listings of art exhibitions and cultural activities in the community

b. What kinds of products are offered?
    1) furniture   2) mobile phones   3) hardware

c. What kinds of services are available?
    1) offering job training classes
    2) announcing job positions
    3) locating qualified employees for companies

d. If you are searching for a house to rent, which link should you go to?
    1) link 7   2) link 6   3) link 2

e. If you are thinking of meeting more friends, which link would help you?
    1) link 8   2) link 4   3) link 1

8.2.5. 課堂口語活動（课堂口语活动）

A. Do you have a page on MySpace, Facebook, or other social-networking Web sites? If the answer is yes, show your class your Web site. Explain what information is on the page and why you want to post it there. If the answer is no, explain why you do not want to have your personal information posted on the social-networking Web sites.

B. Imagine that you find yourself unable to access the Internet and instant messaging, for a week during the semester. What would you do? How would you feel? Prepare a short speech about this situation.

C. A new way of writing English, "cyber writing," has emerged in e-mails and instant messages. Examples include "r u there?", "wuzup?" or no usage of capital letters. Think of other examples. Describe the characteristics of cyber writing. Does cyber writing extend to your other writing in daily life? Do you think the new way of writing will eventually change how English sentences will be written? Discuss these questions in small groups and have a representative report your group's opinions to the whole class.

8.2.6. 看圖寫作（看图写作）： The four pictures tell a story. Imagine you are reporting the story to a friend. Write down the complete story as suggested by the pictures. Give your story a beginning, a middle part and and end.

8.2.7. 寫作（写作）

A. In 8.2.3 Wang Desheng wrote an e-mail to Da Wei, telling Da Wei about the Internet cafés in China. Write an e-mail message on behalf of Da Wei to Wang Desheng including replying to the questions that Wang Desheng asked in his e-mail, based on your own experience.

B. Many experts have claimed that the proliferation of writing, in all its hurried, hasty forms in e-mails and instant messages has actually created a generation more adept with the written word and improved the quality of young people's composition. Do you agree with such a claim? Does frequent writing of e-mails and instant messages help you write and think faster? How is e-mail/IM writing similar to or different from your regular composition? Write an article to express your views on this topic.

第十課　　迎新春

10.1. 迎新春（迎新春）

10.1.1. 生詞練習（生词练习）

A. 迎新春、過聖誕節時人們做什麼？
迎新春、过圣诞节时人们做什么？

Check the following activities that people do for the Chinese New Year or Christmas.

	春節 春节	聖誕節 圣诞节
祭祖	☐	☐
贈送禮物（赠送礼物）	☐	☐
裝飾聖誕樹（装饰圣诞树）	☐	☐
貼春聯（贴春联）	☐	☐
拿紅包（拿红包）	☐	☐
佈置聖誕燈（布置圣诞灯）	☐	☐
大掃除（大扫除）	☐	☐
拜年	☐	☐
辦年貨（办年货）	☐	☐
吃年夜飯（吃年夜饭）	☐	☐
家人團圓（家人团圆）	☐	☐

B. 填空： Here are Li Zhen's comments about Chinese New Year's Eve. Fill in the appropriate words from the list below to complete the paragraph.

壓歲錢，貼春聯，紅包，除夕，熱鬧，過春節，團圓，年糕，年夜飯
压岁钱，贴春联，红包，除夕，热闹，过春节，团圆，年糕，年夜饭

今天晚上是_____，我們全家人_____在一起吃_____。我家的大圓桌上擺滿了媽媽燒的菜，有雞、鴨、魚、肉，還有我最愛吃的_____。吃過晚飯後，爸爸和媽媽忙著在大門上_____，爺爺和奶奶把我叫到一邊給了我一個_____，他們說這是我的_____，不可以馬上用掉，要等到明天再打開。晚上，很多人在外邊放鞭炮，好_____，我真喜歡_____。

★★★★★

今天晚上是_____，我们全家人_____在一起吃_____。我家的大圆桌上摆满了妈妈烧的菜，有鸡、鸭、鱼、肉，还有我最爱吃的_____。吃过晚饭后，爸爸和妈妈忙着在大门上_____，爷爷和奶奶把我叫到一边给了我一个_____，他们说这是我的_____，不可以马上用掉，要等到明天再打开。晚上，很多人在外边放鞭炮，好_____，我真喜欢_____。

C. 簡答題（简答题）： Provide a short answer in Chinese for each of the following questions.

a. 什麼日子讓你等不及，希望那一天快一點到來？
　　什么日子让你等不及，希望那一天快一点到来？

b. 華人過春節是什麼時候大掃除？
   华人过春节是什么时候大扫除？

c. 華人拜年時，互相說什麼？
   华人拜年时，互相说什么？

d. 每個重大的節日都有由來 (*origin*)，聖誕節紀念什麼？
   每个重大的节日都有由来 (*origin*)，圣诞节纪念什么？

e. 你希望今年的聖誕節或生日能得到什麼禮物？
   你希望今年的圣诞节或生日能得到什么礼物？

f. 華人過春節怎麼佈置家裏？
   华人过春节怎么布置家里？

g. 你的祖先是從哪來的？
   你的祖先是从哪来的？

h. 你父母外出讓你一個人看家時，他們通常會告訴你什麼事你千萬
   不能做？
   你父母外出让你一个人看家时，他们通常会告诉你什么事你千万
   不能做？

i. 美國人過西方新年有什麼傳統？
   美国人过西方新年有什么传统？

j. 你通常怎麼表達對一個人的感謝？
   你通常怎么表达对一个人的感谢？

10.1.2. 聽力（听力）: Listen to the conversations and complete the rejoinders. You will hear two short conversations or parts of conversations followed by four choices, designated (A), (B), (C), and (D). Choose the one that continues or completes the conversation in a logical and culturally appropriate manner.

   1. (   ) 2. (   )

10.1.3. 短文閱讀 （短文阅读）： Xiao Yu and her mother both keep diaries. Answer the following multiple-choice questions based on their diary entries on February 5.

小玉和媽媽的日記

小玉的日記

　　春節快到了，媽媽每天下班不是忙著打掃房間就是出去辦年貨。今天吃晚飯的時候也沒有回來。我跟爸爸隨便煮了一些泡麵吃。八點半媽媽回來了，買了大包小包很多東西，有祭祖的祭品，幾幅春聯，還有我愛吃的年糕和魚肉。其實我最關心的是媽媽買了裝壓歲錢的紅包沒有。我在袋子裏找來找去也沒有找到。媽媽是買了不讓我看見，還是她忘了呢？

★ ★ ★ ★ ★

媽媽的日記

　　再幾天就要過春節了，家裡打掃得還不夠徹底，小玉的房間和書房還沒有來得及打掃。年貨已經辦得差不多了，不過還得買青菜和水果，還要叫小玉去給她爺爺和奶奶買毛衣和襪子，再給她的叔叔和伯伯們發電子郵件，請他們除夕晚上都到家裡來吃年夜飯。加上小玉，晚輩們一共有八個孩子。我得記得去銀行領錢，好給孩子們壓歲錢。過春節時，不管多忙我都高興。盼望一家人一年裡平平安安，順順利利。

a. What did Xiao Yu's mom do this evening?
   1) She cleaned Xiao Yu's grandparents' house.
   2) She bought gifts for relatives.
   3) She bought food for New Year's Eve.
   4) She stayed late in her office.

b. What did Xiao Yu find in the shopping bags?
   1) sweaters and socks
   2) food used for paying respect to the ancestors
   3) cleaning products
   4) instant noodles

小玉和妈妈的日记

小玉的日记

　　春节快到了，妈妈每天下班不是忙着打扫房间就是出去办年货。今天吃晚饭的时候也没有回来。我跟爸随便煮了一些泡面吃。八点半妈妈回来了，买了大包小包很多东西，有祭祖的祭品，几幅春联，还有我爱吃的年糕和鱼肉。其实我最关心的是妈妈买了装压岁钱的红包没有。我在袋子里找来找去也没有找到。妈妈是买了不让我看见，还是她忘了呢？

★ ★ ★ ★ ★

妈妈的日记

　　再几天就要过春节了，家里打扫得还不够彻底，小玉的房间和书房还没有来得及打扫。年货已经办得差不多了，不过还得买青菜和水果，还要叫小玉去给她爷爷和奶奶买毛衣和袜子，再给她的叔叔和伯伯们发电子邮件，请他们除夕晚上都到家里来吃年夜饭。加上小玉，晚辈们一共有八个孩子。我得记得去银行领钱，好给孩子们压岁钱。过春节时，不管多忙我都高兴，盼望一家人一年里平平安安，顺顺利利。

c. What did Xiao Yu unsuccessfully try to find in the bag?
1) spring couplets
2) food
3) red envelopes
4) presents for her grandparents

d. What else does Xiao Yu's mom have to do before Chinese New Year?
1) go to the bank to get cash
2) buy more spring couplets for the house
3) call family members to bring their children for a big family gathering
4) e-mail family members to have New Year's Eve dinner at the grandparents' house

10.1.4. 口語回答（口语回答）: For the speech sample, you will need to answer six questions. After you hear each question, you have twenty seconds to record your response. For each question, you should respond as fully and as appropriately as possible.

10.1.5. 課堂口語活動（课堂口语活动）

A. 看圖説話（看图说话）

在台北過春節（在台北过春节）: Sarah is in an exchange program in Taipei during the spring semester. She is living with her host family, the Wangs. Based on the drawings, describe her experiences of celebrating Chinese New Year.

B. Chinese New Year is approaching and your class would like to celebrate the holiday. Work with your classmates in small groups to discuss ideas on how to decorate the classroom and what activities you would like to do during the Chinese New Year. After your discussion, each group will share their ideas with the class. The whole class should finalize and implement the plan.

10.1.6. 寫作（写作）

A. Describe one of your experiences from the holiday season. It could be your favorite Christmas, Hanukkah, or Kwanzaa. It could be anywhere, such as at school, a friend's house, or in a restaurant. You also can dig out some of your photos to go with the text.

B. You all have the experience of celebrating New Year's Eve. How is it different from Chinese New Year? Based on your own experience and the knowledge you learned from the unit, write a paragraph on the similarities and the differences between these two holiday celebrations.

10.2. 春節的故事和風俗（春节的故事和风俗）

10.2.1. 生詞練習（生词练习）

A. 重組（重组）：The following ten sentences describe the story of Nian 年. However, currently the ten sentences are in random order. Read the sentences carefully and reorder them into a logical story line. Place the numbers 1 through 10 in the brackets to indicate the order. The beginning of the story is marked.

（　） 於是家家戶戶都在大門上貼紅紙，在家門前點爆竹。
　　　　于是家家户户都在大门上贴红纸，在家门前点爆竹。

（ 1 ） 很久很久以前傳說有一個怪獸叫「年」，樣子很嚇人。
　　　　很久很久以前传说有一个怪兽叫「年」，样子很吓人。

（　） 以後年獸就再也不敢到村子裡去了。
　　　　以后年兽就再也不敢到村子里去了。

（　） 而貼春聯和放鞭炮的風俗就一直保留到今天。
　　　　而贴春联和放鞭炮的风俗就一直保留到今天。

（　） 有一天村民終於想出對付年獸的辦法。
　　　　有一天村民终于想出对付年兽的办法。

（　） 他們發現年獸見不得紅色，害怕爆炸聲。
　　　　他们发现年兽见不得红色，害怕爆炸声。

（　） 每到除夕，年肚子餓了就出來傷害人，村民都怕得不得了。
　　　　每到除夕，年肚子饿了就出来伤害人，村民都怕得不得了。

（　） 果然，年獸被紅紅的紙和爆竹聲嚇跑了。
　　　　果然，年兽被红红的纸和爆竹声吓跑了。

（　） 年獸很會睡覺，一睡就是三百六十四天。
　　　　年兽很会睡觉，一睡就是三百六十四天。

（　） 後來過春節也叫做過年。
　　　　后来过春节也叫做过年。

B. 完成句子: Complete each of the following sentences to make a coherent statement.

a. 我的弱點是… (我的弱点是…)

_____

b. 不管發生什麼事… (不管发生什么事…)

_____

c. 學校終於放寒假了… (学校终于放寒假了…)

_____

d. 這個電影挺嚇人的… (这个电影挺吓人的…)

_____

e. 他的電腦常識很豐富… (他的电脑常识很丰富…)

_____

C. 吉祥話（吉祥话）: Check the four-word phrases in the following list that are auspicious expressions heard during the Chinese New Year.

a. ❑ 人人皆知

b. ❑ 平安如意

c. ❑ 迎春納福（迎春纳福）

d. ❑ 紀念表演（纪念表演）

e. ❑ 炮竹嚇人（炮竹吓人）

f. ❑ 家家戶戶（家家户户）

g. ❑ 恭喜發財（恭喜发财）

h. ❑ 輕鬆一下（轻松一下）

i. ❑ 年年有餘（年年有余）

D. 簡答題（简答题）: Provide a simple answer in Chinese to each of the following questions.

a. 美國人怎麼慶祝七月四日國慶日？
   美国人怎么庆祝七月四日国庆日？

b. 年夜飯為什麼有吃魚的風俗？
   年夜饭为什么有吃鱼的风俗？

c. 你最喜歡什麼樣的表演？
   你最喜欢什么样的表演？

d. 你們家誰的電腦常識最豐富？
   你们家谁的电脑常识最丰富？

e. 十二生肖的第一個動物是什麼？
   十二生肖的第一个动物是什么？

10.2.2. 聽力（听力）

A. You will hear a phone message for Zhao Lin. Listen to the message and relay the message to Zhao Lin through an e-mail.

B. Listen to the conversations and complete the rejoinders. You will hear two short conversations or parts of conversations followed by four choices, designated (A), (B), (C), and (D). Choose the one that continues or completes the conversation in a logical and culturally appropriate manner.

1. (   )   2. (   )

10.2.3. 短文閱讀（短文阅读）: This is a story of the Chinese zodiac. Based on the story, answer the following questions.

十二生肖的故事

中國人選了十二種動物作為生肖。為什麼老鼠是第一個？為什麼沒有貓呢？ 這是有個故事的。很久很久以前，有一天玉皇大帝對所有的動物說：「我要選出十二種動物，叫做十二生肖，這十二種動物每年輪流當一年的大王。」於是玉皇大帝舉行「過河比賽」來選動物，最先游過河的十二種動物，就被選為十二生肖。貓有點擔心，就對牠的好朋友老鼠說：「我不太會游泳，怎麼辦呢？」老鼠說：「不要緊，老牛很會游泳，可以請他背我們兩個游過去啊！」 比賽那天，老牛游得最快，坐在牛背上的鼠，忽然起了壞主意，把身邊的貓推進水裏，看到老牛快上岸時，馬上從牛背上跳下，於是老鼠成了第一個上河岸的動物，等到貓游到河岸時，十二個動物已經選出來了。從此以後，老鼠永遠是貓的敵人。

a. What did the mouse do?
   1) It helped the cat.
   2) It swam very fast.
   3) It tricked the ox.
   5) It jumped from the horse's back.

b. What did the ox do?
   1) It came in second in the race because it waited for the cat.
   2) It let the mouse win first place.
   3) It tried to help the mouse and the cat.
   4) It taught the mouse how to swim fast.

c. What happened to the cat?
   1) It was pushed into the river.
   2) It came in second in the race because it didn't swim fast enough.
   3) It was out of the race because it did not follow the rules.
   4) It was the last of the twelve animals because it did not know how to swim.

10.2.3. 短文阅读: This is a story of the Chinese zodiac. Based on the story, answer the following questions.

十二生肖的故事

中国人选了十二种动物作为生肖。为什么老鼠是第一个？为什么没有猫呢？ 这是有个故事的。很久很久以前，有一天玉皇大帝对所有的动物说：「我要选出十二种动物，叫做十二生肖，这十二种动物每年轮流当一年的大王。」于是玉皇大帝举行「过河比赛」来选动物，最先游过河的十二种动物，就被选为十二生肖。猫有点担心，就对牠的好朋友老鼠说：「我不太会游泳，怎么办呢？」老鼠说：「不要紧，老牛很会游泳，可以请他背我们两个游过去啊！」 比赛那天，老牛游得最快，坐在牛背上的老鼠忽然起了坏主意，把身边的猫推进水里，看到老牛快上岸时，马上从牛背上跳下，于是老鼠成了第一个上河岸的动物，等到猫游到河岸时，十二个动物已经选出来了。从此以后，老鼠永远是猫的敌人。

a. What did the mouse do?
1) It helped the cat.
2) It swam very fast.
3) It tricked the ox.
6) It jumped from the horse's back.

b. What did the ox do?
1) It came in second in the race because it waited for the cat.
2) It let the mouse win first place.
3) It tried to help the mouse and the cat.
4) It taught the mouse how to swim fast.

c. What happened to the cat?
1) It was pushed into the river.
2) It came in second in the race because it didn't swim fast enough.
3) It was out of the race because it did not follow the rules.
4) It was the last of the twelve animals because it did not know how to swim.

10.2.4. 實文閱讀（实文阅读）: Answer the following questions, based on the flyer represented below.

紐約華人春節聯誼會 　一年一度的春節即將到來，法拉盛華人社區將於二月十七日星期六，在法拉盛希爾頓飯店宴會廳舉辦春節聯誼會。聯誼會內容有歌舞表演、京劇清唱、流行樂曲演奏等。演出結束後，有晚宴、舞會和贈送抽獎禮物。敬請各界人士光臨。 時間：晚上六點三十分到午夜十二點 票價：$25、$50、$100 訂位請電：（718）888-9833	纽约华人春节联谊会 　一年一度的春节即将到来，法拉盛华人社区将于二月十七日星期六，在法拉盛希尔顿饭店宴会厅举办春节联谊会。联谊会内容有歌舞表演、京剧清唱、流行乐曲演奏等。演出结束后，有晚宴、舞会和赠送抽奖礼物。敬请各界人士光临。 时间：晚上六点三十分到午夜十二点 票价：$25、$50、$100 订位请电：（718）888-9833

a. Where is the event going to take place?
   1) a Chinese community center
   2) a university activity center
   3) a hotel
   4) a club

b. Which activity will start first?
   1) dinner
   2) performance
   3) dance
   4) raffle

c. What activities and programs are part of this social function? (check all the correct ones)
   1) Beijing opera
   2) lion dance
   3) auction
   4) games
   5) dancing
   6) dinner
   7) music performance

10.2.5. 課堂口語活動（课堂口语活动）

A. Describe the important holidays in the United States. Divide students into groups. Each group chooses one holiday, such as Independence Day, Halloween, Thanksgiving, Easter, Labor Day, and Memorial Day. In groups, students discuss the significance of the holiday, the activities that people commonly engage in, and the customs followed on that particular holiday. After group discussion, each group selects a student to present the celebrations of that holiday to the class.

Independence Day 美國國慶（美国国庆）
Easter Day 復活節（复活节）
Labor Day 勞工節（劳工节）
Halloween 萬聖節（万圣节）
Thanksgiving Day 感恩節（感恩节）

B. You read several spring couplets in 10.2.6 in the textbook. Do research on the Internet and find a couplet that you like. Find out the meaning of the couplet and present it to the class.

10.2.6. 看圖寫作（看图写作）: The four pictures tell a story. Imagine you are reporting a story to a friend. Write down the complete story as suggested by the pictures. Give your story a beginning, a middle development and an end.

10.2.7. 寫作 （写作）

A. Your Chinese pen pal is coming to study abroad in the United States and will spend a special holiday with her American host family. She wants you to tell her the customs and tradition of celebrations for this particular holiday and remind her what she should know and prepare for. Write a short note to help your Chinese friend get some cultural background.

B. You just came back from studying abroad in China. It is approaching Chinese New Year. A local Chinese newspaper invites you to comment on the similarities and the differences between Chinese New Year and Christmas from the perspective of an American high school student. Write a short article comparing these two holidays.

第十一課　娛樂與藝術
第十一課　娱乐与艺术

11.1.1.生詞練習（生词练习）

A. 解釋詞語（解释词语）：a through **h** are definitions for words in the box. For each definition, choose an appropriate word to fill in the blank.

商場，連續劇，演員，休閒娛樂，郊外，接待，交響樂，美術館
商场，连续剧，演员，休闲娱乐，郊外，接待，交响乐，美术馆

a.＿＿＿＿＿＿＿　　很多樂器演奏的大型樂曲
　　　　　　　　　　很多乐器演奏的大型乐曲

b.＿＿＿＿＿＿＿　　可以看很多名畫和藝術品的地方
　　　　　　　　　　可以看很多名画和艺术品的地方

c.＿＿＿＿＿＿＿　　以演戲為職業的人
　　　　　　　　　　以演戏为职业的人

d.＿＿＿＿＿＿＿　　離市區很遠的地方
　　　　　　　　　　离市区很远的地方

e.＿＿＿＿＿＿＿　　有很多商店的地方

f.＿＿＿＿＿＿＿　　工作結束以後做一些活動讓身心愉快
　　　　　　　　　　工作结束以后做一些活动让身心愉快

g.＿＿＿＿＿＿＿　　招待客人，為客人安排活動
　　　　　　　　　　招待客人，为客人安排活动

h.＿＿＿＿＿＿＿　　分段播放的電視戲劇
　　　　　　　　　　分段播放的电视戏剧

B. 填空:. Jiazhen is talking about the soap opera that she watched last night. Use the vocabulary words in the box to fill in the blanks in the following passage

新聞，欣賞，精彩，流行歌手，古典音樂，睡著
新闻，欣赏，精彩，流行歌手，古典音乐，睡着

昨天晚上的連續劇真是_____。我最_____那位演_____的男演員了，他歌唱得真好聽。連平常只看_____、愛聽_____的姐姐也說這個連續劇太棒了。不過，哥哥不太喜歡看浪漫劇情片，因此看到一半就_____了。

★ ★ ★ ★

昨天晚上的连续剧真是_____。我最_____那位演_____的男演员了，他歌唱得真好听。连平常只看_____、爱听_____的姐姐也说这个连续剧太棒了。不过，哥哥不太喜欢看浪漫剧情片，因此看到一半就_____了。

C. 完成句子: Choose an appropriate word from the box to complete each of the following sentences.

節目，體驗，嚐嚐，主意，博物館，值得，烤肉，原因，安排
节目，体验，尝尝，主意，博物馆，值得，烤肉，原因，安排

a. 好不容易買到票去看那場歌劇，我竟然睡著了，真是不_____！
   好不容易买到票去看那场歌剧，我竟然睡着了，真是不_____！

b. 台灣的姐妹校十月來參觀，接待他們的活動該怎麼_____？
   台湾的姐妹校十月来参观，接待他们的活动该怎么_____？

c. 「早晨公園」有新聞又有音樂，是很不錯的電視_____。
　　「早晨公园」有新闻又有音乐，是很不错的电视_____。

d. 「水煮魚」是四川有名的小吃，一定要_____。
　　「水煮鱼」是四川有名的小吃，一定要_____。

e. 昨天爺爺把幾幅他收藏了很久的山水畫送給了_____。
　　昨天爷爷把几幅他收藏了很久的山水画送给了_____。

f. 咱們到商場去嚐嚐不同口味的烤肉，這個_____怎麼樣？
　　咱们到商场去尝尝不同口味的烤肉，这个_____怎么样？

g. 到華人朋友家過春節是對中華文化最好的_____。
　　到华人朋友家过春节是对中华文化最好的_____。

h. 我們全家週末常到郊外去_____。
　　我们全家周末常到郊外去_____。

i. 這個搖滾樂團的曲子常常創新，是他們受到歡迎的_____。
　　这个摇滚乐团的曲子常常创新，是他们受到欢迎的_____。

11.1.2. 聽力（听力）: Listen to the conversations and complete the rejoinders. You will hear two short conversations or parts of conversations followed by four choices, designated (A), (B), (C), and (D). Choose the one that continues or completes the conversation in a logical and culturally appropriate manner.

1. (　　)　　2. (　　)

11.1.3. 短文閱讀（短文阅读）: Xiaoming is sending an e-mail to his friend, Wang Lihong, telling him that this Saturday he will be unable go to the movie they had planned to see that day. Read the passage then answer the following questions.

立宏:

你好。很抱歉，這個星期六我大概沒辦法跟你去看電影了。 我的時間表排得滿滿的，早上起來得先去博物館，我每個星期六都去那兒當義工。十一點鐘到我父母的餐館去幫忙招待客人和聽電話。下午我答應陪女朋友去大商場給她姐姐買結婚禮物，接著我們要去參加學校舉辦的郊外烤肉活動。晚上我們還要去聽一個演唱會，歌手是楚天和他的搖滾樂團，是我女朋友買的票，我不能不去。不過，我們還多買了一張票，你有興趣一塊兒去嗎？請儘快告訴我。至於那部電影，咱們過幾天再去看吧。

小明

立宏:

你好。很抱歉，这个星期六我大概没办法跟你去看电影了。 我的时间表排得满满的，早上起来得先去博物馆，我每个星期六都去那儿当义工。十一点钟到我父母的餐馆去帮忙招待客人和听电话。下午，我答应陪女朋友去大商场给她姐姐买结婚礼物，接着我们要去参加学校举办的郊外烤肉活动。晚上我们还要去听一个演唱会，歌手是楚天和他的摇滚乐团，是我女朋友买的票，我不能不去。不过，我们还多买了一张票，你有兴趣一块儿去吗？请尽快告诉我。至于那部电影，咱们过几天再去看吧。

小明

---

a. Why can't Xiaoming go to a movie with Lihong today?
  1) He needs to go to the shopping center with his girlfriend.
  2) He has a lunch date with his parents.
  3) He volunteers at a concert.
  4) He is helping with a school activity.

b. What are Xiaoming's plans in the afternoon?
  1) buy a wedding gift
  2) attend a concert
  3) organize an outdoor BBQ event
  4) entertain family guests

c. What is Xiaoming's suggestion?
1) Buy one more ticket for Lihong tonight.
2) Watch the movie when it is on TV.
3) Lihong must see the performance!
4) Go to the concert together.

11.1.4. 口語回答（口语回答）: You will participate in a simulated conversation with Pan Rong, on Skype. She is your Chinese friend in Nanjing, whom you met when you studied abroad there last year. You two are chatting about pastimes. Each time when it is your turn to speak, you will have twenty seconds to respond. You should respond as fully and as appropriately as possible. There will be six times when it is your turn to speak.

11.1.5. 課堂口語活動（课堂口语活动）

A. 看圖説話（看图说话）
約翰的休閒娛樂（约翰的休闲娱乐）: Describe John's favorite pastime based on the drawings.

B. 美國高中生的休閒娛樂 (美国高中生的休闲娱乐)：A group of students from Taiwan is visiting your school. You have been asked by your school to give a short speech describing the pastimes that U.S. high school students enjoy. Also explain why those pastimes are so popular.

11.1.6. 寫作（写作）

A. What is the ultimate concert that you wish to attend? Describe that concert and what you expect to see, hear, and feel there. Also, explain why you are crazy about the singer and/or the band and why the music is special to you.

B. Your sister high school in China plans to buy several TV shows from the United States that will help their students learn the English language and American culture. Divide the class into small groups. Each group discusses the options and suggests a TV show that will help the students in China learn the language and culture. Each group presents their suggestion by describing what the show is about and the reasons for the choice.

11.2. 藝術（艺术）

11.2.1. 生詞練習 （生词练习）

A. 對京劇、歌劇、音樂劇的認識（对京剧、歌剧、音乐剧的认识）：
List at least three words or phrases to describe what you know about Chinese opera, Western opera, and musicals.

京劇(京剧)	
歌劇(歌剧)	
音樂劇(音乐剧)	

B. 反義詞（反义词）： Find an appropriate antonym from the box and fill it in the blank for each of the words.

> 人物，誇張，跌倒，新聞，原因，精彩，郊外，寫實，休閒，古典
> 人物，夸张，跌倒，新闻，原因，精彩，郊外，写实，休闲，古典

a. 時髦 （时髦） _____ f. 抽象 _____

b. 東西 （东西） _____ g. 站好 _____

c. 枯燥無味（枯燥无味）_____ h. 工作 _____

d. 歷史 （历史） _____ i. 都市 _____

e. 結果 （结果） _____ j. 保守 _____

C. 填空: Luo Manling is writing to her pen pal in California about the Beijing opera presentation at her school. Fill in appropriate words from the list to complete the following paragraph.

| 忠心，誇張，情節，人物，抽象，正直，舞台 |
| 忠心，夸张，情节，人物，抽象，正直，舞台 |

上個星期學校請了一個京劇演員給我們做示範演出。他說京劇的表現是＿＿＿＿＿的，不是寫實的，比如說＿＿＿＿＿上沒有很多道具，演員以＿＿＿＿＿的動作，臉譜的顏色和唱詞來表達＿＿＿＿＿。他談到京劇臉譜的顏色象徵＿＿＿＿＿的個性。紅色代表＿＿＿＿＿，白色代表奸詐，黑色代表＿＿＿＿＿。說明完以後，他還表演了一段精彩的美猴王。

★ ★ ★ ★ ★

上个星期学校请了一个京剧演员给我们做示范演出。他说京剧的表现是＿＿＿＿＿的，不是写实的，比如说＿＿＿＿＿上没有很多道具，演员以＿＿＿＿＿的动作，脸谱的颜色和唱词来表达＿＿＿＿＿。他谈到京剧脸谱的颜色象征＿＿＿＿＿的个性。红色代表＿＿＿＿＿，白色代表奸诈，黑色代表＿＿＿＿＿。说明完以后，他还表演了一段精彩的美猴王。

D. 連連看（连连看）： Match each of the words on the left with an appropriate definition on the right.

a. 忠心 　　　自己去經歷，試試看（自己去经历，试试看）

b. 正直 　　　電影或電視劇的故事（电影或电视剧的故事）

c. 情節 　　　像真實的情形一樣，不誇張（像真实的情形一样，不夸张）

d. 體驗 　　　不說假話，不拍馬屁（不说假话，不拍马屁）

e. 道具 　　　真心，不二心

f. 生活化 　　舞臺上演員用的東西（舞台上演员用的东西）

11.2.2. 聽力（听力）

A. Xiao Li left a message for Mark. Listen to the phone message and choose the correct answers for the following questions.

    a. Why did Xiao Li call Mark?
        1) to remind him that they meet at 2:00
        2) to tell him about the festival in the gallery
        3) to let Mark know about the Shanghai Museum
        4) to inform Mark that he bought student tickets

    b. Which statement is true regarding the festival?
        1) It was organized by the Shanghai Museum.
        2) Visitors can learn how to write their names with brushes.
        3) All festival tickets are half-price on Saturday.
        4) Visitors can see how to do paper-cutting.

B. Listen to the conversations and complete the rejoinders. You will hear two short conversations or parts of conversations followed by four choices, designated (A), (B), (C), and (D). Choose the one that continues or completes the conversation in a logical and culturally appropriate manner.

    1. (   )   2. (   )

11.2.3. 短文閱讀（短文阅读）: Chen Li was your Chinese roommate in a summer camp last year in Beijing. Here is an e-mail from her. Write an e-mail to respond to her questions.

你好，

有件事想請教你。我得寫一篇英文報告，比較東西方藝術的差別。我想討論京劇和歌劇的異同。你記不記得有一次我們一起去看京劇，你說中國有京劇，西方有歌劇。京劇類似西方的歌劇嗎？還是差別很大？你喜歡歌劇嗎？為什麼喜歡或者不喜歡？我想聽聽你的看法。

陳莉

你好，

有件事想请教你。我得写一篇英文报告，比较东西方艺术的差别。我想讨论京剧和歌剧的异同。你记不记得有一次我们一起去看京剧，你说中国有京剧，西方有歌剧。京剧类似西方的歌剧吗？还是差别很大？你喜欢歌剧吗？为什么喜欢或者不喜欢？我想听听你的看法。

陈莉

11.2.4. 實文閱讀（实文阅读）： Choose correct answers for the following multiple-choice questions based on the authentic reading.

武漢電視臺節目表 七月十二日　星期四	武汉电视台节目表 七月十二日　星期四
17:00 焦點訪談：臺灣民間藝術家	17:00 焦点访谈：台湾民间艺术家
17:30 新娛樂：流行歌曲前十名	17:30 新娱乐：流行歌曲前十名
18:00 美食天地：烤肉	18:00 美食天地：烤肉
18:30 比賽精選：國際網球決賽	18:30 比赛精选：国际网球决赛
19:30 法律常識：買屋賣屋	19:30 法律常识：买屋卖屋
20:00 連續劇：夢想成真	20:00 连续剧：梦想成真
21:00 晚間新聞	21:00 晚间新闻
22:00 古典之音：貝多芬的交響曲	22:00 古典之音：贝多芬的交响曲

a. If you like symphonic music, when should you turn to this TV station?
   1) 5:30 pm
   2) 7:30 pm
   3) 8:00 pm
   4) 10:00 pm

b. What will you see on this TV station at 5:00 pm?
   1) the evening news
   2) a soap opera
   3) a program about Taiwan society
   4) an interview with an artist

c. The gourmet cooking program is scheduled
   1) right before the soap opera
   2) between a music and a sports program
   3) after the news
   4) right after a documentary

11.2.5. 課堂口語活動（课堂口语活动）

A. In 11.2 of the textbook, several Chinese traditional arts are introduced, such as puppet shows, embroidery, ink painting, paper-cutting, Chinese knots, Beijing opera, etc. Your class decides to gain further understanding of Chinese traditional arts. Divide the class into small groups and have each group choose a Chinese traditional art. It can be one of the areas mentioned in the textbook or an art you find on your own. The group's task is to find information about the selected traditional art. Make a group presentation for the whole class and include a poster.

B. A group of Chinese students will participate in the summer camp at your high school. Your class is asked to give a presentation to them regarding American music, dance, and other arts. Each group should selects an area of interest. Suppose your group decides to present "tap dancing." Do research on "tap dancing" to find out its origin, history, development, and well-known dancers. Each group should present its findings with PowerPoint slides.

11.2.6. 看圖寫作（看图写作）： The following four pictures tell a story. Imagine you are writing the story to a friend. Narrate a complete story as suggested by the pictures. Give your story a beginning, a middle part, and an end.

11.2.7. 寫作 （写作）

A. You are applying for a summer job as a counselor for the Chinese Culture and Art Camp for elementary school children. You are required to write an essay to explain why you choose this job and how you will help children experience Chinese culture and art to meet the camp's expectations. Use as much vocabulary from the lesson as possible.

B. Your pen pal in China is coming to visit you this summer for a week. Write a letter to welcome him and tell him about the local attractions as well as your arrangements for his one-week stay. Also, ask him what things and activities he would like to see and do.

第十二課　　從四合院到摩天大樓
第十二課　　从四合院到摩天大楼

12.1. 房子：郊區與市區（房子：郊区与市区）

12.1.1. 生詞練習（生词练习）

A. 解釋詞語（解释词语）: a through **g** are definitions for the words in the box. For each definition, choose an appropriate word to place on the corresponding line.

> 價錢，車庫，鄰居，交通，超級市場，捨不得，公共設施
> 价钱，车库，邻居，交通，超级市场，舍不得，公共设施

a. ＿＿＿＿＿＿＿　　停放車子的地方
　　　　　　　　　　停放车子的地方

b. ＿＿＿＿＿＿＿　　大家都可以使用的設備或地方
　　　　　　　　　　大家都可以使用的设备或地方

c. ＿＿＿＿＿＿＿　　可以在這裡買到吃的和用的東西
　　　　　　　　　　可以在这里买到吃的和用的东西

d. ＿＿＿＿＿＿＿　　馬路上車輛來來往往的情形
　　　　　　　　　　马路上车辆来来往往的情形

e. ＿＿＿＿＿＿＿　　住在你家四周圍的人家
　　　　　　　　　　住在你家四周围的人家

f. ＿＿＿＿＿＿＿　　買某種物品需要付的錢數
　　　　　　　　　　买某种物品需要付的钱数

g. ＿＿＿＿＿＿＿　　不願意放棄，想要一直留著
　　　　　　　　　　不愿意放弃，想要一直留着

B. 填空: Ling Ling and David have both moved to new homes. The following passages are their comments with respect to their new lives and homes. Fill in appropriate words to complete the paragraphs.

a. Ling Ling talks about how her father goes to work every day.

> 地鐵，擁擠，計程車，空氣，新鮮，附近，塞車
>
> 地铁，拥挤，计程车，空气，新鲜，附近，塞车

　　我家現在住在紐約市＿＿＿＿的小城裏，因為離海邊很近，所以＿＿＿很＿＿＿＿。我也非常喜歡我的新學校。但是住在這個新家，父親每天去紐約上班不太方便。他每天坐＿＿＿＿，車上常常很＿＿＿＿＿，如果開車上班，公路經常＿＿＿＿，搭＿＿＿＿上班又太貴了，很不實際。我知道父親為我和媽媽付出了很多，我應該對父親更好些。

★ ★ ★ ★ ★

　　我家现在住在纽约市＿＿＿＿的小城里，因为离海边很近，所以＿＿＿很＿＿＿＿。我也非常喜欢我的新学校。但是住在这个新家，父亲每天去纽约上班不太方便。他每天坐＿＿＿＿，车上常常很＿＿＿＿＿，如果开车上班，公路经常＿＿＿＿，搭＿＿＿＿上班又太贵了，很不实际。我知道父亲为我和妈妈付出了很多，我应该对父亲更好些。

b. David is commenting on his family's new home.

> 房子，各式各樣，公寓，特色，大樓，搬家
> 房子，各式各样，公寓，特色，大楼，搬家

　　我們又＿＿＿＿＿了，這次從芝加哥的市區搬到了加州的郊區，這真讓我不習慣。芝加哥有＿＿＿＿＿的摩天大樓，我們的＿＿＿＿＿在一棟＿＿＿＿＿裡，從上面往下看，市區的全景很有＿＿＿＿＿，尤其是夜景。現在我家雖然是加州郊區的一棟新＿＿＿＿＿，可是看起來和左右鄰居們的房子一模一樣，我放學回家的時候，差一點找不著家了。

★ ★ ★ ★ ★

　　我们又＿＿＿＿＿了，这次从芝加哥的市区搬到了加州的郊区，这真让我不习惯。芝加哥有＿＿＿＿＿的摩天大楼，我们的＿＿＿＿＿在一栋＿＿＿＿＿里，从上面往下看，市区的全景很有＿＿＿＿＿，尤其是夜景。现在我家虽然是加州郊区的一栋新＿＿＿＿＿里，可是看起来和左右邻居们的房子一模一样，我放学回家的时候，差一点找不着家了。

12.1.2. 聽力 （听力）: Listen to the conversations and complete the rejoinders. You will hear two short conversations or parts of conversations followed by four choices, designated (A), (B), (C), and (D). Choose the one that continues or completes the conversation in a logical and culturally appropriate manner.

1. (　　)　　2. (　　)

12.1.3. 短文閱讀（短文阅读）： Tai Sheng's family just moved. He expresses his feelings about his new surroundings below. Select correct answers for the following multiple-choice questions based on his writing.

上個月因為父親工作的關係，我們從臺北搬到了美國東部的一個小城裏。這裡的風景好是好，可是對我來說實在是太過於安靜了。在臺北，我聽慣了市區汽車、摩托車、公車的喇叭聲，坐在公寓三樓的家裏，城市的交通交響樂是我生活的一部分，戴上耳機一邊聽音樂一邊做功課，感覺非常好。現在住在這麼安靜的地方，尤其是父母都很晚下班，我家的院子前後沒有鄰居，我反而不能安心地做功課。

★ ★ ★ ★ ★

上个月因为父亲工作的关系，我们从台北搬到了美国东部的一个小城里。这里的风景好是好，可是对我来说实在是太过于安静了。在台北，我听惯了市区汽车、摩托车、公车的喇叭声，坐在公寓三楼的家里，城市的交通交响乐是我生活的一部分，戴上耳机一边听音乐一边做功课，感觉非常好。现在住在这么安静的地方，尤其是父母都很晚下班，我家的院子前后没有人，我反而不能安心地做功课。

---

a. What reason did Tai Sheng give for his family's move?
   1) They moved to a city apartment in the eastern United States.
   2) His parents enjoy the beauty of small towns, so they decided to move.
   3) They wanted to move to a small town to escape city life.
   4) They relocated to the United States because of his father's job.

b. What is his impression about the new place?
   1) very remote
   2) very spacious
   3) very quiet
   4) very boring

c. What does Tai Sheng think about life in Taipei?
   1) The city is bustling.
   2) The transportation is convenient.
   3) The apartments do not have yards.
   4) His parents did not work late.

12.1.4. 口語回答（口语回答）: You will participate in a simulated conversation with a Chinese friend, Zhang Gutong, who just arrived in the United States. Out of curiosity, she is asking you some questions about the housing environment here. Each time when it is your turn to speak, you will have twenty seconds to respond. You should respond as fully and as appropriately as possible. There will be six times when it is your turn to speak.

12.1.5. 課堂口語活動（课堂口语活动）

A. 看圖說話（看图说话）

我家的新房子（我家的新房子）:

B. Your class decides to have a Dream House Design Competition. The dream house can be located anywhere in the world. Each student makes a poster with drawings of his or her dream house. In the oral report, explain the design of the house layout, as well as the environment, location, and community where you choose to build the house.

12.1.6. 寫作（写作）

A. You will study abroad next semester in Beijing. Your Chinese host family would like to know more about you and your family. In addition to family photos, you plan to show them the house your family lives in by making a scrapbook. Take some photos of the inside and outside of your parents' house, and write a couple of lines to describe each photo. Be sure to include at least one photo in which you can describe a memorable event happening in your house. Use as many words as you can from 12.1.

B. Choose a place where you would like to live and work after graduating from college. Search online and find an apartment or house that you like. Write a paragraph explaining the reasons you want to live there and describing the size, style, price, rooms, facilities, and the environment of the apartment or house. Include the images from the Internet.

12.2. 歷史遺產四合院（历史遗产四合院）

12.2.1. 生詞練習 （生词练习）

A. 解釋生詞（解释生词）: **a** to **f** are definitions for the words in the box. For each definition, choose an appropriate word to place on the corresponding line.

> 目前，方式，消失，隨處可見，價值，如何
> 目前，方式，消失，随处可见，价值，如何

a. _____ 現在、最近的這段時間
　　　　　　　　　現在、最近的这段时间

b. _____ 走到哪裡都能看見
　　　　　　　　　走到哪里都能看见

c. _____ 怎麼樣(怎么样)

d. _____ 說話或做某事情的方法和形式
　　　　　　　　　说话或做某事情的方法和形式

e. _____ 不見了(不见了)

f. _____ 商品所值的錢數；常是指用途或重要性
　　　　　　　　　商品所值的钱数；常是指用途或重要性

B. 反義字 (反义字): Choose an antonym from the box for each of the following words. Write the antonym in the blank.

> 進步，消失，熱鬧，推動，附近，剩下，願意，目前
> 进步，消失，热闹，推动，附近，剩下，愿意，目前

a. 停下(停下)_____　　　e. 落後(落后)_____

b. 不要(不要)_____　　　f. 遙遠(遥远)_____

c. 冷清(冷清)_____　　　g. 出現(出现)_____

d. 用完(用完)_____　　　h. 過去(过去)_____

C. 填空: Zeng Shi is expressing his opinion about the traditional-style houses in Beijing. Fill in appropriate words from the list to complete the following paragraph.

推動保護，經濟發展，要不然，價值，四合院，改建，消失
推动保护，经济发展，要不然，价值，四合院，改建，消失

如果你有機會去北京，一定要去看看很有中國特色的_____。隨著中國_____，很多四合院被拆除了，人們把原有的四合院_____成了摩天大樓。因此積極_____四合院是目前重要的工作，_____這種具有藝術_____的歷史遺產就會慢慢_____了。

★ ★ ★ ★ ★

如果你有机会去北京，一定要去看看很有中国特色的_____。隨着中国_____，很多四合院被拆除了，人们把原有的四合院_____成了摩天大楼。因此积极_____四合院是目前重要的工作，_____这种具有艺术_____的历史遗产就会慢慢_____了。

D. 填空: Zhao Tong advocates protecting the courtyard house by renovating and updating their appearance and function. Fill in appropriate words from the list to complete the following paragraph.

剩下，遺產，如何，建議，進步，願意，落後，貧窮
剩下，遗产，如何，建议，进步，愿意，落后，贫穷

有人_____把所有的老房子都拆掉，改變城市_____和_____的面貌。他們認為新的摩天大樓就是_____的象徵。我不同意這種說法。老房子，尤其是四合院，是中華歷史文化的

_____，現在_____的已經是為數不多了。_____讓老房子改換新貌、加以利用，又不丟掉原有的藝術價值，是對城市建築的挑戰，但是這是我們應該做的。任何中國人都不_____四合院的獨特風貌被摩天大樓取代了。

★★★★★

有人_____把所有的老房子都拆掉，改變城市_____和_____的面貌。他们认为新的摩天大楼就是_____的象征。我不同意这种说法。老房子，尤其是四合院，是中华历史文化的_____，现在_____的已经是为数不多了。_____让老房子改换新貌、加以利用，又不丢掉原有的艺术价值，是对城市建筑的挑战，但是这是我们应该做的。任何中国人都不_____四合院的独特风貌被摩天大楼取代了。

12.2.2. 聽力（听力）

A. You will hear a brief report from a city planner in Beijing to a group of architects and developers, then be asked to answer some true/false questions. Circle T or F for the following statements based on the report.

    a. T/F   The city planner suggested that the crowdedness in the city can be solved by renovating the old buildings into residential housing.

    b. T/F   More residential housing should be built in the suburbs.

    c. T/F   To save space, the city has decided to develop some underground parking lots.

    d. T/F   There are no concrete plans yet for preserving courtyard house.

B. Listen to the conversations and complete the rejoinders. You will hear two short conversations or parts of conversations followed by four choices, designated (A), (B), (C), and (D). Choose the one that continues or completes the conversation in a logical and culturally appropriate manner.

    1. (   )   2. (   )

12.2.3. 短文閱讀（短文阅读）：Your Chinese pen pal Dong Jianmin wrote you the following e-mail. Read the e-mail then write a response to him.

尼克：

很久沒跟你聯絡了，你都好嗎？

我們家最近剛搬家，搬到一棟有八層樓的公寓裡。雖然水電、衛浴設備都很齊全，但我還是不太習慣公寓的環境，鄰居之間互相不認識。聽說美國家庭通常住在房子而不住在公寓裡，是真的嗎？為什麼？你們家也住房子嗎？你喜不喜歡現在住的地方？你們常常跟鄰居來往嗎？

我們公寓最大的好處就是附近有地鐵，到什麼地方都很方便。你的城市有地鐵嗎？交通方不方便？對了，你會開車嗎？有沒有你自己的車？美國孩子真幸運，十六歲就可以開車了！

尼克：

很久没跟你联络了，你都好吗？

我们家最近刚搬家，搬到一栋有八层楼的公寓里。虽然水电、卫浴设备都很齐全，但我还是不太习惯公寓的环境，邻居之间互相不认识。听说美国家庭通常住在房子而不住在公寓里，是真的吗？为什么？你们家也住房子吗？你喜不喜欢现在住的地方？你们常常跟邻居来往吗？

我们公寓最大的好处就是附近有地铁，到什么地方都很方便。你的城市有地铁吗？交通方不方便？对了，你会开车吗？有没有你自己的车？美国孩子真幸运，十六岁就可以开车了！

12.2.4. 實文閱讀（实文阅读）：This is a typical courtyard house. Some parts of the house layout are labeled with names in Chinese. Answer the following five questions based on the drawing.

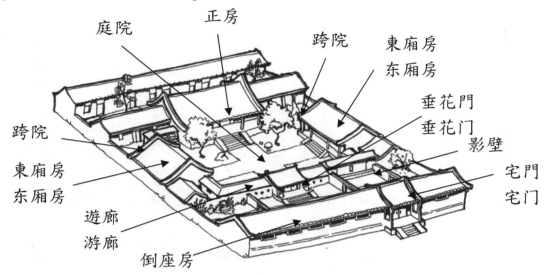

庭院　正房　跨院　東廂房 东厢房　垂花門 垂花门　影壁　宅門 宅门

跨院　東廂房 东厢房　遊廊 游廊　倒座房

1 · Which is the entrance of the house?

2 · Which room is for the master of the house?

3 · Which two rooms are for the other family members?

4 · How many entrances does the house have?

5 · What does 遊廊 (游廊) mean?

12.2.5. 課堂口語活動（课堂口语活动）

A. Your school is celebrating International Culture Festival next month. Each class will present a project showing the diversity of culture and traditions in the world. Your class plans to do a project on traditional housing and architecture in different cultures. Pair up with a classmate. Each pair does research and chooses one form of traditional housing or architecture. The final product can be a poster or PowerPoint presentation, demonstrating the house or building with necessary labels in Chinese. In the oral report, each pair describes and explains the historical background and the unique features of the traditional architecture.

B. You are a supporter of preserving traditional houses and buildings. In order to convince people that preservation tasks can coexist with economic development and modernization, you decide to do research on successful cases in various parts of the world. Make an oral presentation to your class on a successful case of historic preservation that you have found and read about.

12.2.6. 看圖寫作（看图写作）: The four pictures tell a story. Imagine you are writing the story to a friend. Narrate a complete story as suggested by the pictures. Give your story a beginning, a middle part, and an end.

12.2.7. 寫作（写作）

A. In lesson 12 of the textbook, you learned the Chinese saying "A close neighbor is better than a distant relative." Provide an example that you have experienced or you have heard that reflects this Chinese saying.

B. In section 12.2.1 of the textbook, you read about the traditional courtyard house in Beijing, some of its architectural features, and advocacy for protecting it. About the courtyard house, you want to learn more about courtyard house and the current state of those houses. Do research on the courtyard house and write a paper including (1) the history of the courtyard house, (2) life in a specific courtyard house, (3) architectural features that are not mentioned in lesson 12, and (4) current plans to preserve the courtyard house.

第十三課　留學
第十三课　留学

13.1. 談留學（谈留学）

13.1.1. 生詞練習（生词练习）

A. 留學應該考慮的因素（留学应该考虑的因素）： When planning to study in China or Taiwan, which of the following factors should be considered first?

☐薪水高低　　　　　　　　　☐接待家庭

☐學習目標（学习目标）　　　☐宿舍的大小

☐文化課程（文化课程）　　　☐網路（网络）

☐說中文的機會（说中文的机会）　☐學費高低（学费高低）

B. 簡答題（简答题）： Answer the following questions.

a. 留學時跟接待家庭住在一起有很多好處。請舉一個例子。
   留学时跟接待家庭住在一起有很多好处。请举一个例子。

b. 現在有哪些電視節目的觀眾對象是高中學生？
   现在有哪些电视节目的观众对象是高中学生？

c. 你學習中文是以什麼為目標？
   你学习中文是以什么为目标？

d. 甚麼活動你很想試試看，但是一直沒有時間或者機會？
   甚么活动你很想试试看，但是一直没有时间或者机会？

e. 留學時，對於接待家庭的選擇，你會考慮哪些因素？
   留学时，对于接待家庭的选择，你会考虑哪些因素？

f. 假設你有機會到臺灣或中國留學，除了學習語言以外，另外你還想學什麼？
   假设你有机会到台湾或中国留学，除了学习语言以外，另外你还想学什么？

C. 填空: Fill in appropriate words from the lists to complete the following two paragraphs.

a. David's Chinese teacher is telling the class about study abroad programs.

項目，強調，對象，國際，因素，著重，運用，考慮，目的
項目，強調，对象，国际，因素，着重，运用，考虑，目的

　　為了幫助對中文有興趣的＿＿＿＿＿學生，近年來臺灣和中國開設了不少的留學＿＿＿＿＿　。根據教學＿＿＿＿＿和＿＿＿＿＿，有的項目＿＿＿＿＿口語，有的提供實習機會，讓學生＿＿＿＿＿所學。有的＿＿＿＿＿文化知識的獲得。當你做留學計畫時，一定要＿＿＿＿＿這些＿＿＿＿＿。

★ ★ ★ ★ ★

　　为了帮助对中文有兴趣的＿＿＿＿＿学生，近年来台湾和中国开设了不少的留学＿＿＿＿＿　。根据教学＿＿＿＿＿和＿＿＿＿＿，有的项目＿＿＿＿＿口语，有的提供实习机会，让学生＿＿＿＿＿所学。有的＿＿＿＿＿文化知识的获得。当你做留学计划时，一定要＿＿＿＿＿这些＿＿＿＿＿。

b. Mary is explaining to a new exchange student in her class how to follow class rules.

強調，提出，樂意，當然，儘管
强调，提出，乐意，当然，尽管

　　老師一再＿＿＿＿＿，如果你有問題，要等到她說完話以後再＿＿＿＿＿，她會很＿＿＿＿＿回答。＿＿＿＿＿，如果真有緊急事情，也可以＿＿＿＿＿提出，不要擔心。

★★★★★

老师一再＿＿＿＿＿＿＿，如果你有问题，要等到她说完话以后再＿＿＿＿＿＿＿，她会很＿＿＿＿＿＿＿回答。＿＿＿＿＿＿＿，如果真有紧急事情，也可以＿＿＿＿＿＿＿提出，不要担心。

13.1.2. 聽力（听力）： Listen to the conversations and complete the rejoinders. You will hear two short conversations or parts of conversations followed by four choices, designated (A), (B), (C), and (D). Choose the one that continues or completes the conversation in a logical and culturally appropriate manner.

1. (　　) 2. (　　)

13.1.3. 短文閱讀（短文阅读）： The following is a flyer for a summer Chinese language program. Based on the flyer, choose the best answer for each of the following questions.

中文項目

對象：	高中生，十六歲以上，對中文有興趣的人士
地點：	西安
時間：	六月二十五日至八月二十四日止 (八星期)
費用：	2,000 美元, 包括學費、教材、旅遊交通費、食宿費
旅遊：	秦俑博物館和附近名勝古跡，北京三天二夜遊
住宿安排：	學校宿舍，中國同屋，二週的時間與接待家庭同住
教學方式：	根據學生程度分班教學，小班制，每班最多六個人。強調聽說讀寫。

課程

初級班：	強調發音、口語、認字和中國文化
中級班：	中級口語、閱讀、中國文化及風俗習慣，學習中國成語及歷史故事。著重閱讀。
高級班：	高級口語、閱讀、寫作、辯論及演講。著重寫作。

中文项目

对象：	高中生，十六岁以上，对中文有兴趣的人士
地点：	西安
时间：	六月二十五日至八月二十四日止 (八星期)
费用：	2,000 美元,包括学费、教材、旅游交通费、食宿费
旅游：	秦俑博物馆和附近名胜古迹，北京三天二夜游
住宿安排：	学校宿舍，中国同屋，二周的时间与接待家庭同住
教学方式：	根据学生程度分班教学，小班制，每班最多六个人。强调听说读写。

课程

初级班：	强调发音、口语、认字和中国文化
中级班：	中级口语、阅读、中国文化及风俗习惯，学习中国成语及历史故事。着重阅读。
高级班：	高级口语，阅读，写作、辩论及演讲。着重写作。

a. Who is eligible to participate in this studying abroad program?
   1) 16 to 18 year olds
   2) 24 year olds
   3) 16 year olds and those older
   4) anyone interested in learning Chinese

b. What is the housing arrangement for the students?
   1) They will live in a rental apartment.
   2) They will stay with a host family for eight weeks
   3) They will stay four weeks with a host family, four weeks in a school dormitory.
   4) They will have a Chinese roommate.

c. Which level includes historical stories?
   1) beginner
   2) intermediate
   3) advanced
   4) all levels

13.1.4. 口語回答（口语回答）： You will participate in a simulated conversation with Mr. Ma Fengda on the phone. He is your host family father in Taipei. Each time it is your turn to speak, you will have twenty seconds to respond. You should respond as fully and as appropriately as possible. There will be six times when it is your turn to speak.

13.1.5. 課堂口語活動（课堂口语活动）
A. 看圖說話（看图说话）

瑪莉的留學經驗（玛莉的留学经验）：Describe Mary's experience of study in Hualian based on the drawings.

B. 留學計畫（留学计划）：Students are divided into small groups and do research on various kinds of study abroad programs in China or Taiwan. Each group chooses a program and presents the program, describing details of the program (such as location, curriculum, tour, tuition, accommodations, etc.), explaining why the program interests the group, and what you can learn from the study abroad experience.

13.1.6. 寫作（写作）

A. Your grandparents will pay for your study abroad program as a graduation gift after you graduate in June next year. This is a wonderful opportunity for you to pursue your dreams. What kind of program would you like to choose? Write a paragraph including the details of your plan and explain why you want to do those activities. Use the words in the box in your writing.

> 接待家庭，項目，著重，目的，運用，因素，考慮
>
> 接待家庭，项目，着重，目的，运用，因素，考虑

B. Interview a person who has had the experience of study abroad. That person can be your friend, teacher, relative, or parent. Find out why he or she decided to study abroad and how the experience was. Ask him or her to give you advice in planning to study abroad in the future. Write a short article based on what you have found out.

13.2. 在中國、臺灣留學（在中国、台湾留学）

13.2.1. 生詞練習（生词练习）

A. 解釋生詞（解释生词）: a to **f** are definitions for the words in the box. Find and fill in an appropriate word from the list for each definition.

> 緊湊，了若指掌，流利，和藹可親，密集式，名勝古蹟，夫婦
> 紧凑，了若指掌，流利，和蔼可亲，密集式，名胜古迹，夫妇

a. （　　）　一個接著一個發生，中間不停止
　　　　　　　一个接着一个发生，中间不停止

b. （　　）　有名的風景區，有歷史價值的地方
　　　　　　　有名的风景区，有历史价值的地方

c. （　　）　說得很通順，很快
　　　　　　　说得很通顺，很快

d. （　　）　連續上幾個小時的課
　　　　　　　连续上几个小时的课

e. （　　）　先生和太太

f. （　　）　對人很溫和親切
　　　　　　　对人很温和亲切

g. （　　）　了解得很清楚
　　　　　　　了解得很清楚

B. 反義字(反义字): Choose an antonym from the list for each of the following words. Write the antonym in the blank.

> 害怕，脫，緊湊，細節，親切，密集
> 害怕，脱，紧凑，细节，亲切，密集

a.輕鬆（轻松）　_____　　　d.冷淡　_____

b.重點（重点）　_____　　　e.勇敢　_____

c.分散　_____　　　　　　　f.穿　_____

C. 填空: Fill in appropriate words from the lists to complete the following two paragraphs. Mark's experiences studying abroad with his class are described here.

> 曬，禮金，空調，適應，脫鞋，親切，甜點，訓練，婚禮
> 晒，礼金，空调，适应，脱鞋，亲切，甜点，训练，婚礼

去年夏天馬克在上海留學一個月，接待家庭對他很 _____，帶他參觀名勝古跡。他也參加了一個 _____。馬克注意到華人參加婚禮時不送禮物給新人，而是送 _____。他也注意到中國人的習慣是進門要 _____，衣服 _____在陽臺上，飯後吃水果不吃 _____，還有 _____只在最熱的時候才打開。馬克認為留學生活可以 _____獨立以及 _____新環境的能力。

★★★★★

去年夏天马克在上海留学一个月，接待家庭对他很 _____，带他参观名胜古迹。他也参加了一个 _____。马克注意到华人参加婚礼时不送礼物给新人，而是送 _____。他也注意到中国人的习惯是进门要 _____，衣服 _____在阳台上，饭后吃水果不吃 _____，还有 _____只在最热的时候才打开。马克认为留学生活可以 _____独立以及 _____新环境的能力。

D. 回答問題（回答问题）：Answer the following questions.

a. 列出下面三個地方的名勝古蹟（列三個）
   列出下面三个地方的名胜古迹（列三个）

美國/美国			
臺灣/台湾			
中國/中国			

b. 華人在生活習慣上跟美國人有什麼不一樣？
   华人在生活习惯上跟美国人有什么不一样？

1. _____

2. _____

3. _____

c. 當你去留學時，你要怎麼適應新的環境？
   当你去留学时，你要怎么适应新的环境？

1. _____

2. _____

3. _____

13.2.2. 聽力（听力）

A. You will hear a welcome speech to the new students from the director of the study abroad program. Choose the correct answers for the following questions based on the speech.

    a. How long does the program last?
1) four weeks
2) eight weeks
3) one semester
4) one year

    b. What is the subject in the morning?
1) intensive Mandarin Chinese
2) Mandarin Chinese and calligraphy
3) Mandarin Chinese and martial arts
4) individual practice with the instructor

    c. What are the activities being offered Friday evening?
1) free time
2) eating at a Chinese restaurant and then singing karaoke
3) watching Chinese movies and drinking tea
4) learning folk dances and martial arts

    d. What is the special arrangement during the fourth week?
1) going to a night market
2) watching a Chinese cooking show during dinner
3) various sports competitions
4) staying with a host family after school

B. Listen to the conversations and complete the rejoinders. You will hear two short conversations or parts of conversations followed by four choices, designated (A), (B), (C), and (D). Choose the one that continues or completes the conversation in a logical and culturally appropriate manner.

      1. (   )   2. (   )

13.2.3. 短文閱讀（短文阅读）： Your Chinese friend Zhou Kai wrote you the following e-mail. Read the e-mail and write a response to her.

丹娜：

　　聽說你要來臺灣留學我很高興。我也希望有機會到美國去進修英文，跟美國同學交流。可不可以麻煩你幫我找找資料？你們的社區有沒有學校開設短期的英文班？有哪些課程？怎麼申請？不知道能不能安排接待家庭？你覺得如果我跟美國家庭同住會不會有困難？對了，如果你對到臺灣留學有什麼問題，儘管問我。

周凱

丹娜：

　　听说你要来台湾留学我很高兴。我也希望有机会到美国去进修英文，跟美国同学交流。可不可以麻烦你帮我找找资料？你们的社区有没有学校开设短期的英文班？有哪些课程？怎么申请？不知道能不能安排接待家庭？你觉得如果我跟美国家庭同住会不会有困难？对了，如果你对到台湾留学有什么问题，尽管问我。

周凯

13.2.4. 實文閱讀（实文阅读）

西安秦俑博物館實習報名簡章

日期：	七月十五日至八月十五日
時間：	上午八點至下午四點
課程：	上午學習中國歷史、考古課程、參觀秦俑博物館，下午實習如何修補秦俑。晚上欣賞傳統音樂和舞蹈表演或自由活動。
費用：	美金兩千元
報名日期：	五月二十日止
報名方式：	網上報名，網址: xianqinyong@yahoo.com

西安秦俑博物馆实习报名简章

日期：	七月十五日至八月十五日
时间：	上午八点至下午四点
课程：	上午学习中国历史、考古课程、参观秦俑博物馆，下午实习如何修补秦俑。晚上欣赏传统音乐和舞蹈表演或自由活动。
费用：	美金两千元
报名日期：	五月二十日止
报名方式：	网上报名，网址: xianqinyong@yahoo.com

---

a. What does this flyer announce?
1) a language study abroad program
2) a cultural tour
3) an internship opportunity
4) a summer job

b. What will students learn from the program?
1) to restore terra-cotta warriors
2) to excavate terra-cotta warriors
3) to make terra-cotta warriors
4) to study the sites where terra-cotta warriors were excavated

13.2.5. 課堂口語活動（课堂口语活动）

A. Role-play (with a partner): You are being interviewed for a full scholarship to cover the expenses of studying Chinese in Taiwan, China, or Singapore for one year. One student will be the interviewer and the other student will be the interviewee. The interviewer must address the following questions when interviewing the interviewee.

    a. Why are you interested in studying Chinese?
    b. At which location do you wish to study Chinese? Why did you choose this place?
    c. What language skills would you like to focus on?
    d. What kinds of cultural activities would you like to experience?
    e. How will this experience change your life?

B. You are selected to study Chinese in China. You have the choice of staying either in a school dormitory or with a host family. Explain to the class why you would prefer to stay at a school dormitory or with a host family.

13.2.6. 看圖寫作（看图写作）

The four pictures tell a story. Imagine you are writing the story to a friend. Narrate a complete story as suggested by the pictures. Give your story a beginning, a middle part, and an end.

13.2.7. 寫作（写作）

A. You are the director for an international program that sends students to study abroad. Your job is to design a flyer that will encourage high school students to sign up for your program. Your flyer should include where the students will go abroad, the cost, the housing accommodations, curriculum and activities, etc.

B. You are going to study abroad in Nanjing for six months. You hope you can stay with a host family for the entire period. You wish you can get along with your host family and that your host family will help you improve your Chinese language skills. You also hope the host family can take you to visit scenic spots and historical sites. Write a letter to the director who matches students with their host families and let him or her know your wishes. Use the words in the box.

> 夫婦，和藹可親，親切，害怕，名勝古蹟，流利
> 夫妇，和蔼可亲，亲切，害怕，名胜古迹，流利

14.1. 旅遊（旅游）

14.1.1. 生詞練習（生词练习）

A. 旅遊準備（旅游准备）：Check the words below that are related to traveling abroad for a vacation.

a. ❏ 護照（护照）　　　　　　f. ❏ 獎學金（奖学金）

b. ❏ 軟體（软体）　　　　　　g. ❏ 時差（时差）

c. ❏ 政治　　　　　　　　　　h. ❏ 導遊（导游）

d. ❏ 制服　　　　　　　　　　i. ❏ 旅行社

e. ❏ 簽證（签证）　　　　　　j. ❏ 教材

B. 填空：Changsong just returned from a trip to Africa. Fill in appropriate words from the list to complete the following paragraph.

氣候，風景，費用，探險，轉機，簽證，生產
我跟爸爸剛剛從非洲東岸的肯尼亞＿＿＿＿＿＿回來。我想寫一篇文章敘述這一次的旅行經過。那個地方秋天＿＿＿＿＿＿優美，＿＿＿＿＿＿宜人，讓我留下了深刻的印象。肯尼亞生產咖啡和蔗糖，還有很多野生動物。雖然辦＿＿＿＿＿＿的＿＿＿＿＿＿很貴，要一百塊，而且坐飛機還得＿＿＿＿＿＿，不能直飛到那兒，可是非常值得去看看。

气候，风景，费用，探险，转机，签证，生产
我跟爸爸刚刚从非洲东岸的肯尼亚_____回来。我想写一篇文章叙述这一次的旅行经过。那个地方秋天时_____优美，_____宜人，让我留下了深刻的印象。肯尼亚生产咖啡和蔗糖，还有很多野生动物。虽然办_____的_____很贵，要一百块，而且坐飞机还得_____，不能直飞到那儿，可是非常很值得去看看。

C. 下面這些城市哪些在臺灣？請打✓。哪些在中國？請打〇。
　　下面这些城市哪些在台湾？请打✓。哪些在中国？请打〇。

蘇州，臺北，花蓮，青島，廣州，台東， 西安，臺中，臺南，北京，烏魯木齊 ★★★★★ 苏州，台北，花莲，青岛，广州，台东， 西安，台中，台南，北京，乌鲁木齐

D. 詞語解釋（词语解释）：**a** to **f** are definitions for the words in the box. Choose and fill in the appropriate word to match with each of the definitions.

> 沿海，信用卡，入境，旅行社，商業，亞洲
> 沿海，信用卡，入境，旅行社，商业，亚洲

a. _____ 專門替人買飛機票或安排行程的地方
　　　　　　　　　专门替人买飞机票或安排行程的地方

b. _____ 日本、中國、臺灣所在的大陸
　　　　　　　　　日本、中国、台湾所在的大陆

c. _____ 從外國進入另一個國家
　　　　　　　　　从外国进入另一个国家

d. _____ 購物時，方便用來付錢的證件
　　　　　　　　　购物时，方便用来付钱的证件

e. _____ 做買賣的活動
　　　　　　　　　做买卖的活动

f. _____ 不在內地，在海邊
　　　　　　　　　不在内地，在海边

14.1.2. 聽力（听力）：Listen to the conversations and complete the rejoinders. You will hear two short conversations or parts of conversations followed by four choices, designated (A), (B), (C), and (D). Choose the one that continues or completes the conversation in a logical and culturally appropriate manner.

　　1. (　　) 2. (　　)

14.1.3. 短文閱讀（短文阅读）： Read Wensheng's travelogue and answer the following questions.

文生的遊記

七月七日：從紐約出發，先到達東京，再飛香港轉機。很累！下午到新加坡。為了省旅館費用，當天坐夜車從新加坡到馬來西亞。

七月八日：火車穿過馬來西亞半島，可惜晚上看不見車外優美的風景。一路睡得很舒服，連飯都沒吃。

七月九日：從馬來西亞首都吉隆坡坐飛機到越南首都胡志明市。飛機又快又舒服。天氣又悶又熱。

七月十日：在胡志明市的街道上隨便走走。很多建築很有法國情調。小店賣的咖啡味道非常好。

七月十一日：從胡志明市坐飛機直飛雲南昆明。到了昆明，搭長途汽車去麗江和大理。

文生的游记

七月七日：从纽约出发，先到达东京，再非香港转机。下午到新加坡。很累！为了省旅馆费用，当天坐夜车从新加坡到马来西亚。

七月八日：火车穿过马来西亚半岛，可惜晚上看不见车外优美的风景。一路睡得很舒服，连饭都没吃。

七月九日：从马来西亚首都吉隆坡坐飞机到越南首都胡志明市。飞机又快又舒服。天气又闷又热。

七月十日：在胡志明市的街道上随便走走。很多建筑很有法国情调。小店卖的咖啡味道非常好。

七月十一日：从胡志明市坐飞机直飞云南昆明。到了昆明，搭长途汽车去丽江和大理。

---

a. How many means of transportation did Wensheng take during the trip?

b. Wensheng has been to the following cities during this trip. Give the order of the cities visited from 1 to 7 based on his travelogue.

    ____ 香港

    ____ 昆明

    ____ 紐約（纽约）

    ____ 東京（东京）

    ____ 新加坡

    ____ 吉隆坡

    ____ 胡志明市

14.1.4. 口語回答（口语回答）： You will participate in a simulated conversation with Mr. Wang Junshan. He is your travel agent in China. Each time it is your turn to speak, you have twenty seconds to record your response. You should respond as fully and as appropriately as possible. There will be six times when it is your turn to speak.

14.1.5. 課堂口語活動（课堂口语活动）

A. 看圖説話（看图说话）

旅行: Zhang Tong and her friend are taking a trip to Asia. Based on the drawings, describe their experience of the journey.

B. 認識中國和臺灣（认识中国和台湾）：

Each student chooses a city or an area in China or Taiwan. Do research and find out various aspects of that place or area, such as population, geography, weather, agriculture, people, culture, food, scenic spots, historical sites, etc. Use PowerPoint with photos to present the place in class.

14.1.6. 寫作（写作）

A. A Chinese friend plans to come to visit you and study English in your city. She would like to know how to apply for a student visa to the United States, what the expenses and options of living accommodations are, and how convenient public transportation is. She also wishes to know what the weather is like there, and what clothes she should bring if she were to come during the summer. Write her a letter to respond to her questions.

B. Design a travel brochure for a place that you have not been to, but that you would love to take a trip to. Do research on the highlights of that place. Your brochure should describe a weekend plan in that place, including what to do and where to eat and stay. Be creative. The goal of the brochure is to attract tourists' attention!

14.2. 旅遊感想（旅游感想）

14.2.1. 生詞練習（生词练习）

A. 連連看（连连看）： Match the locations on the left with the descriptions on the right.

萬里長城（万里长城）　　　　　　有許多兵馬俑
　　　　　　　　　　　　　　　　有许多兵马俑

阿里山　　　　　　　　　　　　　是西藏文化的象徵
　　　　　　　　　　　　　　　　是西藏文化的象征

秦始皇陵　　　　　　　　　　　　是中國歷史上最偉大的建築
　　　　　　　　　　　　　　　　是中国历史上最伟大的建筑

布達拉宮（布达拉宫）　　　　　　有森林、雲海和日出三大奇觀
　　　　　　　　　　　　　　　　有森林、云海和日出三大奇观

B. 解釋生詞（解释生词）: a to g are the definitions for the words and phrases in the box. Choose a word or phrase and fill it in the blank to match with the definition.

> 雄偉，順利，潮濕，悶熱，努力，積極，繁多
> 雄伟，顺利，潮湿，闷热，努力，积极，繁多

a. ＿＿＿＿＿＿天氣很熱，氣壓低（天气很热，气压低）

b. ＿＿＿＿＿＿肯定的，正面的

c. ＿＿＿＿＿＿很認真地工作（很认真地工作）

d. ＿＿＿＿＿＿建築看起來又高又大（建筑看起来又高又大）

e. ＿＿＿＿＿＿做事沒遇到困難（做事没遇到困难）

f. ＿＿＿＿＿＿花色、類型很多（花色、类型很多）

g. ＿＿＿＿＿＿水分比平常多

C. 簡答題（简答题）： Answer the following questions.

a. 美國最大的三個港口是哪三個？中國的三大港口呢？
   美国最大的三个港口是哪三个？中国的三大港口呢？

b. 中國人口佔世界的百分之多少？
   中国人口占世界的百分之多少？

c. 從經濟方面來說，移民對美國有哪些幫助？
   从经济方面来说，移民对美国有哪些帮助？

d. 現在最流行的服裝是什麼樣的？
   现在最流行的服装是什么样的？

e. 全球化是什麼意思？請舉個例子。
   全球化是什么意思？请举个例子。

f. 眼花撩亂是什麼感覺？你經驗過嗎？請說說看。
   眼花撩乱是什么感觉？你经验过吗？请说说看。

g. 為什麼城市裏應該保留綠地？有什麼好處？
   为什么城市里应该保留绿地？有什么好处？

D. 完成對話（完成对话）： Use the phrase or word in the parenthesis to complete the short exchange.

a. A: 你今天怎麼打扮得這麼漂亮？（感覺）
      你今天怎么打扮得这么漂亮？（感觉）

   B: _____

b. A: 現在市場對什麼的需求最大？（據...說）
      现在市场对什么的需求最大？（据...说）

   B: _____

c. A: 美國的移民還繼續在增加嗎？（隨著）
　　美国的移民还继续在增加吗？（随着）

　　B: _____

d. A: 你考試考得怎麼樣？（反正）
　　你考试考得怎么样？（反正）

　　B: _____

E. 反義字（反义字）: Choose an antonym from the list for each the following words. Write the antonym in the blank.

潮濕，領導，增加，悶熱，需求，繼續
潮湿，领导，增加，闷热，需求，继续

a.減少（减少）　_____　　　d. 停止　　　_____

b.涼快（凉快）　_____　　　e. 跟隨（跟随）_____

c.乾燥（干燥）　_____　　　f. 供給（供给）_____

14.2.2. 聽力（听力）

A. You and your good friend, Liao Xiang, will make a three-week trip to Taipei this summer with a group. The teacher chaperone is sharing information about the trip with your group. Liao Xiang is sick and cannot attend. Listen to the teacher's announcement and then write an e-mail to Liao Xiang to pass on the information to her.

B. Listen to the conversations and complete the rejoinders. You will hear two short conversations or parts of conversations followed by four choices, designated (A), (B), (C), and (D). Choose the one that continues or completes the conversation in a logical and culturally appropriate manner.

　　1.（　）2.（　）

14.2.3. 短文閱讀（短文阅读）：Based on the short reading, choose the correct answer for each of the following questions.

> 　　捷運對臺北市在各方面的影響極大。捷運是臺北人出門最方便的交通工具。捷運讓臺北人減少三分之二的時間在路上，本來半個小時才能到達目的地，現在十分鐘就到了。捷運既準時又乾淨，坐起來非常舒適。乘客只要有捷運路線圖在手，搭車換車都很容易，也不必擔心塞車。由於捷運，臺北市車輛的數量減少，交通的擁擠程度較舒緩，空氣也較為新鮮。捷運也有利於臺北市社區的發展，許多鄉鎮在捷運沿路修建商場、公園以及旅遊景觀，帶動了社區的繁榮。
>
> ★ ★ ★ ★ ★
>
> 　　捷运对台北市在各方面的影响极大。捷运是台北人出门最方便的交通工具。捷运让台北人减少三分之二的时间在路上，本来半个小时才能到达目的地，现在十分钟就到了。捷运既准时又干净，坐起来非常舒适。乘客只要有捷运路线图在手，搭车换车都很容易，也不必担心塞车。由于捷运，台北市车辆的数量减少，交通的拥挤程度较为舒缓，空气也较为新鲜。捷运也有利于台北市社区的发展，许多乡镇在捷运沿路修建商场、公园以及旅游景观，带动了社区的繁荣。

a. If going to a certain destination used to take an hour, approximately how long will it take by MRT?
   1) 10 minutes
   2) 20 minutes
   3) 30 minutes
   4) 40 minutes

b. Besides providing fast transportation, what else does MRT bring to Taipei?
   1) income for the city
   2) better city planning
   3) clean air
   4) foreign tourists

c. MRT also helps
   1) increase property value
   2) decrease the crime rate
   3) lower the ticket prices of public transportation
   4) reduce traffic congestion

14.2.4. 實文閱讀 （实文阅读）

A.

美華大飯店

提供五星級服務。飯店位於上海市中心，交通方便。客房均設有彩色電視、獨立的空調系統、大型書桌、傳真機及電腦插座等。每晚推出國際美食及精彩表演。

★★★★★

美华大饭店

提供五星级服务。饭店位于上海市中心，交通方便。客房均设有彩色电视、独立的空调系统、大型书桌、传真机及电脑插座等。每晚推出国际美食及精彩表演。

B.

好山水之家

座落於臺北國家公園的山間。20間客房。提供舒適的泡湯間。一樓大廳提供客人免費享用的高山茶。餐廳提供山中野菜和放山雞，吃得安心健康，讓您在不知不覺中愛上我們的好山水！

★★★★★

好山水之家

坐落于台北国家公园的山间。20间客房。提供舒适的泡汤间。一楼大厅提供客人免费享用的高山茶。餐厅提供山中野菜和放山鸡，吃得安心健康，让您在不知不觉中爱上我们的好山水！

a. What do the two flyers advertise?
   1) hotels
   2) restaurants
   3) tours
   4) entertainment

b. What is the main difference between the two restaurants described in the flyers?
   1) number of rooms
   2) size of the facilities
   3) services provided
   4) price range

14.2.5. 課堂口語活動（课堂口语活动）

A. 中國、臺灣之旅（中国、台湾之旅）：Students work in pairs to plan a ten-day trip to China with a budget of $3,000, based on information found on the Internet. In the travel plan, each pair has to specify the itinerary and budget, including lodging, transportation, and sightseeing activities as well as the reasons why they want to visit those places. Each pair uses PowerPoint to present their trip.

B. 美國旅遊好去處（美国旅游好去处）：Imagine that your class has been assigned the task of making a presentation on "Travel in the United States" to a group of Chinese visitors. Each of you chooses a place in the United States that you would recommend the Chinese visitors visit. In the presentation, use photos to describe the scenery or the historical or cultural significance of that place and to explain why you think it is worth visiting.

14.2.6. 看圖寫作（看图写作）： The four pictures present two young people's journey. Please write a complete story with a beginning, middle part, and ending based on the four drawings.

14.2.7. 寫作（写作）

A. In 14.2.2 of the textbook, you read a comparison between Shanghai and New York. For this writing assignment, you will choose two cities, one in the United States and one in China or Taiwan. First, do research on the chosen cities. Then, write an article to explain the similarities and differences between the two cities in terms of economy, industry, culture, people, environment, and society. Include any important information that you find.

B. Your Chinese sister school is sending a delegation to your city this month. Your class has been asked to make a booklet about your city for the delegation. The booklet will inform them about the development and history of the city, places to visit (attractions, dining, shopping), and special festivals or events happening this month in your city.

As a class, first decide what should be included in the booklet. Second, students should form small groups with each group choosing a section to focus on. Third, each group should assign a writing task for every individual student. Lastly, the whole class should bind the various sections into a booklet.

第十五課　　海外華人
第十五课　　海外华人

15.1. 華裔美人（华裔美人）

15.1.1. 生詞練習（生词练习）

A. 詞語解釋（词语解释）：**a** to **g** are definitions for the words in the box. Choose and fill in the appropriate word to match each of the definitions.

> 夢想，傑出，寫作，實現，成就，衝突，公民
> 梦想，杰出，写作，实现，成就，冲突，公民

a. ＿＿＿＿＿　跟他人意見不合，發生爭吵
　　　　　　　跟他人意见不合，发生争吵

b. ＿＿＿＿＿　在美國可以投票選參議員的人
　　　　　　　在美国可以投票选参议员的人

c. ＿＿＿＿＿　在工作事業上的表現
　　　　　　　在工作事业上的表现

d. ＿＿＿＿＿　特別突出，不是一般的

e. ＿＿＿＿＿　創作小說的過程
　　　　　　　创作小说的过程

f. ＿＿＿＿＿　把一個夢想完成了
　　　　　　　把一个梦想完成了

g. ＿＿＿＿＿　一個想法，也許是無法實現的
　　　　　　　一个想法，也许是无法实现的

B. 簡答題：簡單回答下面的問題
　　简答题：简单回答下面的问题

a. 你有什麼夢想？
　 你有什么梦想？

b. 海外華人是什麼人？他們有哪國國籍？
　 海外华人是什么人？他们有哪国国籍？

c. 美國允許公民擁有幾個國籍？
美国允许公民拥有几个国籍？

d. 美國有哪些少數民族？臺灣呢？
美国有哪些少数民族？台湾呢？

e. 美國是第幾世紀獨立的？
美国是第几世纪独立的？

C. 填空： The founder of the Hua Feng Art Design Company and his partner are holding an anniversary celebration party with their employees. Use the words in the boxes to complete the following paragraphs.

a. The founder of the Hua Feng Art Design Company gives a brief speech at the party.

理念，實現，創業，堅持，放棄，成立，公司
理念，实现，创业，坚持，放弃，成立，公司

大家好。五年前我有一個夢想，感謝大家的努力，讓我一步一步的＿＿＿＿＿＿了這個夢想。我們華風美術設計＿＿＿＿＿＿經歷了不少＿＿＿＿＿＿的艱難，今天已經＿＿＿＿＿＿整整五年了。我在這裡感謝各位的努力合作。我認為公司的成功是因為我們一直＿＿＿＿＿＿把最好的設計交給顧客。這個＿＿＿＿＿＿保證高品質的服務。請大家無論在什麼情況下都不要＿＿＿＿＿＿這個原則。

★ ★ ★ ★ ★

大家好。五年前我有一个梦想，感谢大家的努力，让我一步一步的＿＿＿＿＿＿了这个梦想。我们华风美术设计＿＿＿＿＿＿经历了不少＿＿＿＿＿＿的艰难，今天已经＿＿＿＿＿＿整整五年了。我在这里感谢各位的努力合作。我认为公司的成功是因为我们一直＿＿＿＿＿＿把最好的设计交给顾客。这个＿＿＿＿＿＿保证高品质的服务。请大家无论在什么情况下都不要＿＿＿＿＿＿这个原则。

b. The partner of the Hua Feng Art Design Company also gives a short speech and mentions that the company is minority run.

夥伴，創新，少數民族，世紀

伙伴，创新，少数民族，世纪

　　我做為這家「華風美術公司」的經濟 _____ ，也想在今天的聚會上說兩句話。很高興我們公司在這五年中不斷 _____ ，有了我們自己的特色。現在我們的顧客越來越多，聲譽越來越好。 地方報上稱我們是美國 _____ 小型企業的代表。希望我們在高科技競爭的新 _____ 裡能更加努力，往前邁進。

★ ★ ★ ★ ★

　　我做为这家「华风美术公司」的经济 _____ ，也想在今天的聚会上说两句话。很高兴我们公司在这五年中不断 _____ ，有了我们自己的特色。现在我们的顾客越来越多，声誉越来越好。 地方报上称我们是美国 _____ 小型企业的代表。希望我们在高科技竞争的新 _____ 里能更加努力，往前迈进。

15.1.2. 聽力（听力）: Listen to the conversations and complete the rejoinders. You will hear two short conversations or parts of conversations followed by four choices, designated (A), (B), (C), and (D). Choose the one that continues or completes the conversation in a logical and culturally appropriate manner.

1. (　　)　　2. (　　)

15.1.3. 短文閱讀（短文阅读）： Wang Tongsheng presents the story of his grandfather to his class. Select the correct answers for the following questions based on his presentation.

各位同學好，今天我要向大家介紹我爺爺在美國的創業史。我爺爺二十世紀初就一個人移民到美國。剛來的時候不會說英文，只能在中國城的飯館裡當廚師，生活充滿了困難，可是他每個月仍寄錢回中國給家人。後來，爺爺發現在美國的華人對中國食品的需求，就和幾位夥伴開了一家食品店，專賣在美國買不到的中國食品。他們的理念是顧客的需要永遠是第一位，所以生意做得很成功。現在我爺爺在美國擁有十三家食品店，2003 年還被選為傑出的華裔美人。爺爺常常告訴我一定要有夢想，才有夢想實現的一天。

各位同学好，今天我要向大家介绍我爷爷在美国的创业史。我爷爷二十世纪初就一个人移民到美国。刚来的时候不会说英文，只能在中国城的饭馆里当厨师，生活充满了困难，可是他每个月仍寄钱回中国给家人。后来，爷爷发现在美国的华人对中国食品的需求，就和几位伙伴开了一家食品店，专卖在美国买不到的中国食品。他们的理念是顾客的需要永远是第一位，所以生意做得很成功。现在我爷爷在美国拥有十三家食品店，2003 年还被选为杰出的华裔美人。爷爷常常告诉我一定要有梦想，才有梦想实现的一天。

a. What kind of business did Mr. Wang's grandfather establish?
1) travel agency   2) restaurant   3) service station   4) food store

b. What is the possible year when his grandfather came to the United States?
1) 1899   2) 1908   3) 1956   4) 1978

c. What did Wang Tongsheng's grandfather tell him?
   1) to have a dream
   2) to work hard and realize his dream
   3) not to daydream of impossible goals
   4) to be a successful Chinese American

d. Which statement is correct, based on Wang Tongsheng's report?
   1) His grandfather came with his family to the United States.
   2) His grandfather is a good cook and received an award for being an outstanding chef.
   3) His grandfather pays attention to the customer's needs.
   4) His grandfather started the business single-handedly.

15.1.4. 口語回答（口语回答）： You will participate in a simulated conversation with an exchange student from China. Each time it is your turn to speak, you have twenty seconds to record your response. You should respond as fully and as appropriately as possible. There will be six times when it is your turn to speak.

15.1.5. 課堂口語活動（课堂口语活动）

A. 看圖說話（看图说话）： Song Guomin came to the United States to study. Based on the drawings, describe his experiences.

B. 美國的少數民族（美国的少数民族）：Divide the students into small groups. Each group chooses one minority, such as Italian Americans, Irish Americans, Chinese Americans, Vietnamese Americans, Korean Americans, Jewish Americans, etc. Do research on that minority group, describing their immigration history, hardships, and achievements. Each group gives a report on their chosen minority.

15.1.6. 寫作（写作）

A. Interview a Chinese American who immigrated to the United States from Taiwan, China, Singapore, or any other country. Find out why he or she came to the United States, the experiences he or she has been through here, the challenges that he or she has had to overcome, and his or her decision to stay here permanently. Write this person's immigration story based on your interview.

B. In textbook lesson 15, you read about the achievements of several Chinese Americans. Choose a famous Chinese American who is successful in his or her profession as mentioned in the lesson. Write that person's success story based on your research. Also, include what you have learned from that person's experience.

15.2. 海外華人（海外华人）

15.2.1. 生詞練習（生词练习)

A. 同義字（同义字）: Choose a synonym from the box for each of the following words. Write the synonym in the blank.

> 家鄉，普通話，大約，遊覽，貿易，觀光客
> 家乡，普通话，大约，游览，贸易，观光客

a.旅遊的人　　_____
　旅游的人

d. 商業（商业）_____

b.漢語（汉语）_____

e. 老家　　　　_____

f. 差不多　　　_____

c.旅行　　　　_____

B. 詞語解釋（词语解释): **a** to **h** are definitions for the words in the box. Choose and fill in an appropriate word to match with each of the definitions.

> 產品，招牌，熟悉，食品，修車，遊覽勝地，角色，展覽
> 产品，招牌，熟悉，食品，修车，游览胜地，角色，展览

a._____　可以去觀看、欣賞藝術品或者新產品的地方
　　　　　　　可以去观看、欣赏艺术品或者新产品的地方

b._____　對一件事情非常了解（对一件事情非常了解）

c._____　工廠製造的東西（工厂制造的东西）

d._____　商店門上頭的板子，寫著商店的名字
　　　　　　　商店门上头的板子，写着商店的名字

e._____　吃的東西（吃的东西）

f._____　電影中的人物（电影中的人物）

g._____　可以去遊玩觀光的地方（可以去游玩观光的地方）

h._____　車子壞了或有問題的時候應該做的事
　　　　　　　车子坏了或有问题的时候应该做的事

C. 完成對話（完成对话）：Use the phrase or word in the parenthesis to complete the short exchange.

a. A: 你喜歡看什麼樣的電影？（對⋯有吸引力）

你喜欢看什么样的电影？（对⋯有吸引力）

B: _____

b. A: 我對這個地方一點也不熟悉？（難怪）

我对这个地方一点也不熟悉？（难怪）

B: _____

c. A: 你住的那一州有多少少數民族？（據估計）

你住的那一州有多少少数民族？（据估计）

B: _____

d. A: 你頭髮實在太長了！什麼時候剪啊？（順便）

你头发实在太长了！什么时候剪啊？（顺便）

B: _____

D. 簡答題（简答题）：Answer the following questions.

a. 你認為個人的健康跟什麼息息相關？
你认为个人的健康跟什么息息相关？

b. 你有沒有「大開眼界」的經驗？請描述一下。
你有没有"大开眼界"的经验？请描述一下。

c. 你認為少數民族在美國社會扮演什麼樣的角色？
你认为少数民族在美国社会扮演什么样的角色？

d. 你喜歡什麼風味的菜？為什麼？
你喜欢什么风味的菜？为什么？

e. 你的家鄉在哪兒？用幾個句子描述你的家鄉。
你的家乡在哪儿？用几个句子描述你的家乡。

15.2.2. 聽力（听力）

A. Your friend is visiting Houston's Chinatown. He left a phone message for you. Listen to the message and select the correct answers for the following questions.

a. What did Daming visit in Houston's Chinatown?
1) Chinese schools
2) a temple
3) a community exhibition
4) a Chinese organization

b. What impression did Daming have of Houston's Chinatown?
1) It is similar to San Francisco's.
2) It is very crowded.
3) Bellaire is the main street.
4) There are a couple of supermarkets.

c. According to Daming,
1) Houston's Chinatown was built more or less at the same time as San Francisco's.
2) Several K—12 public schools in or near Chinatown offer Chinese courses.
3) It is a commercial place and does not have residential areas.
4) Houston Chinatown includes Korean and Vietnamese communities.

d. What was Daming doing, when he was calling?
1) enjoying some Taiwanese food
2) praying in the temple
3) window-shopping
4) drinking Chinese herbal tea

B. Listen to the conversations and complete the rejoinders. You will hear two short conversations or parts of conversations followed by four choices, designated (A), (B), (C), and (D). Choose the one that continues or completes the conversation in a logical and culturally appropriate manner.

1. (   ) 2. (   )

15.2.3. 短文閱讀（短文阅读）：

Please read the following profile of Mr. Leland Yee, who is the first California senator (參議員/参议员) of Asian descent. The information is based on the 7 September 2007 *Sampan* newspaper.

> 余先生是加州第一位亞裔州參議員。余先生 1948 年在中國出生，很小就移民來美，在三藩市唐人街長大，從小學到大學都在舊金山求學，他的博士學位是在夏威夷大學取得的，專長是兒童心理學。在多年的工作中，他對亞裔美人的健康給予極大的關注，並逐漸對政治產生了興趣。身為參議員，余先生重視兒童的教育，積極立法要求電腦遊戲的廠商清楚說明遊戲內容，以便父母可以做正確的選擇。余先生的成功也在於他一心一意為亞裔社區服務，他說："我比任何人都更了解亞裔群體的需求。"
>
>
>
> 余先生是加州第一位亚裔州参议员。余先生 1948 年在中国出生，很小就移民来美，在三藩市唐人街长大，从小学到大学都在旧金山求学，他的博士学位是在夏威夷大学取得的，专长是儿童心理学。在多年的工作中，他对亚裔美人的健康给予极大的关注，并逐渐对政治产生了兴趣。身为参议员，余先生重视儿童的教育，积极立法要求电脑游戏的厂商清楚说明游戏内容，以便父母可以做正确的选择。余先生的成功也在于他一心一意为亚裔社区服务，他说："我比任何人都更了解亚裔群体的需求。"

a.   Mr. Yee is
1) the highest-ranking Asian American elected official in the United States.
2) the first Chinese American senator in the United States.
3) the first Chinese American senator in California.
4) the first Chinese American elected politician in the United States.

b.   Mr. Yee
1) was born in China.
2) grew up in China.
3) received all of his education in San Francisco.
4) came to the United States for his B.A. degree.

c. Mr. Yee's area of specialization for his Ph.D. was in
   1) child psychology.
   2) political science.
   3) immigration law.
   4) education.

d. What is the issue that Mr. Yee has focused on as a senator?
   1) mental health of Asian Americans
   2) restrictions on violent video games for children
   3) political involvement of Asian Americans
   4) the industry of computer games built by Asian Americans

15.2.4. 實文閱讀（实文阅读）： This is a list of new books in a Chinatown bookstore. Choose the correct book for each of the following questions.

華中新書目錄

1. 我是一名華裔美國士兵:第二次世界大戰
2. 家鄉菜餚自己動手
3. 如何通過美國公民入籍考試
4. 唐人街的今昔
5. 創業理念：實現你的夢想

华中新书目录

1. 我是一名华裔美国士兵:第二次世界大战
2. 家乡菜肴自己动手
3. 如何通过美国公民入籍考试
4. 唐人街的今昔
5. 创业理念：实现你的梦想

Questions	book #				
a. Which book teaches cooking?	1	2	3	4	5
b. Which book presents an individual's experience?	1	2	3	4	5
c. Which book helps one become an American citizen?	1	2	3	4	5
d. Which book tells the historical development of an area?	1	2	3	4	5
e. Which book discusses the establishment of a business?	1	2	3	4	5

15.2.5. 課堂口語活動（课堂口语活动）

A. Chinese arrived in the United States in the early nineteenth century. What are the experiences of Chinese Americans in the history of the United States? Divide the class into small groups. Each group does research on the history of Chinese Americans, chooses one aspect to focus on, and reports that aspect to the class.

B. In the United States, we have seen communities established by minorities, such as Chinatown, Koreatown, Little Italy, etc. Divide the class into small groups. Each group should explore the local minority areas by collecting information, visiting those places, and interviewing people. Each group gives a report about that minority community in class.

15.2.6. 看圖寫作（看图写作）: The four pictures tell a story. Imagine you want to narrate a complete story as suggested by the pictures. Give your story a beginning, a middle part, and an end.

15.2.7. 寫作（写作）

A. Your friend in China wrote the following e-mail regarding an American friend that he just met. Write an e-mail to respond to his.

嗨，羅傑：

我昨天在網吧認識了一個從紐約來的美國學生。他提到紐約的中國城，聽起來挺有意思的。你去過紐約的中國城嗎？你覺得怎麼樣？他說很多美國大城市都有中國城，是真的嗎？你住的那個城市有沒有中國城？給我描述一下吧。你們那兒的華人社區大不大？通常有什麼活動？你參加他們的活動，應該對你的中文有幫助吧？對不對？

★ ★ ★ ★ ★

嗨，罗杰：

我昨天在网吧认识了一个从纽约来的美国学生。他提到纽约的中国城，听起来挺有意思的。你去过纽约的中国城吗？你觉得怎么样？他说很多美国大城市都有中国城，是真的吗？你住的那个城市有没有中国城？给我描述一下吧。你们那儿的华人社区大不大？通常有什么活动？你参加他们的活动，应该对你的中文有帮助吧？对不对？

B. In exercise 15.2.5.A, you learned about the past experiences of Chinese Americans in this country. What about Chinese Americans in the current society? Have you noticed the changes? In comparison with other minority groups, such as Hispanics or African Americans, do you find similarities or differences among these groups?

第十六課　　保護瀕臨絕種的動物
第十六課　　保护濒临绝种的动物

16.1. 瀕臨絕種的動物（濒临绝种的动物）

16.1.1. 生詞練習（生词练习）

A. 連連看（连连看）： Match the vocabulary on the left with the description on the right.

a. 獵人（猎人）　　一天比一天多

b. 同伴　　　　　　非常靠近（非常靠近）

c. 消失　　　　　　捕殺動物的人（捕杀动物的人）

d. 遍佈（遍布）　　到處都有（到处都有）

e. 日益　　　　　　一直減少直到什麼都沒有

　　　　　　　　　一直减少直到什么都没有

f. 瀕臨（濒临）　　關於做買賣的事情（关于做买卖的事情）

g. 商業（商业）　　在一起生活或工作的人

B. 反義詞（反义词）： Choose an antonym from the list for each of the following words. Write the antonym in the blank.

> 野外，縮小，優先，大量，破壞，繁殖，特有，污染
> 野外，缩小，优先，大量，破坏，繁殖，特有，污染

a. 保護（保护）＿＿＿＿＿＿＿　　e. 普通＿＿＿＿＿＿＿

b. 少數（少数）＿＿＿＿＿＿＿　　f. 增大＿＿＿＿＿＿＿

c. 乾淨（干净）＿＿＿＿＿＿＿　　g. 家居＿＿＿＿＿＿＿

d. 絕種（绝种）＿＿＿＿＿＿＿　　h. 最後（最后）＿＿＿＿＿＿＿

C. 簡答題（简答题）: Answer the following questions.

   a. 非洲有最多的野生動物。舉三種非洲特有的動物。
       非洲有最多的野生动物。举三种非洲特有的动物。

   b. 臺灣獼猴需要什麼樣的生態環境才能繁殖生長？
       台湾猕猴需要什么样的生态环境才能繁殖生长？

   c. 什麼裝飾品可以放在客廳？舉三個例子。
       什么装饰品可以放在客厅？举三个例子。

   d. 哪些特徵是人類特有而其他動物都沒有的？
       哪些特征是人类特有而其它动物都没有的？

   e. 獵人捕殺大海龜和大象是因為這些動物具有什麼商業價值？
       猎人捕杀大海龟和大象是因为这些动物具有什么商业价值？

D. 填空: Here is an informational display put up by the school's environmental club. Fill in words from the list to complete the information.

> 繁殖，由於，再加上，消失，瀕臨，人類，污染
> 繁殖，由于，再加上，消失，濒临，人类，污染

白頭鷹是美國的象徵。據估計，在十八世紀美國有五十萬隻白頭鷹，五十年代還有十萬隻。白頭鷹的數量減少，最大的敵人就是_____。

_____人類_____環境，破壞生態平衡，白頭鷹的棲息地日益縮小最後_____。白頭鷹因為沒有建築鳥巢的地方，無法_____下一代，_____獵人大量捕殺，到了六十年代只剩下五百隻。一九六七年到一九九五之間，白頭鷹被列為_____絕種的動物。經過各種努力，白頭鷹的數量才逐漸增加。

★★★★★

白头鹰是美国的象征。据估计，在十八世纪美国有五十万只白头鹰，五十年代还有十万只。白头鹰的数量减少，最大的敌人就是_____。_____人类_____环境，破坏生态平衡，白头鹰的栖息地日益缩小最后_____。白头鹰因为没有建筑鸟巢的地方，无法_____下一代，_____猎人大量捕杀，到了六十年代只剩下五百只。一九六七年到一九九五之间，白头鹰被列为_____绝种的动物。经过各种努力，白头鹰的数量才逐渐增加。

16.1.2. 聽力（听力）: Listen to the conversations and complete the rejoinders. You will hear two short conversations or parts of conversations followed by four choices, designated (A), (B), (C), and (D). Choose the one that continues or completes the conversation in a logical and culturally appropriate manner.

1. (   ) 2. (   )

16.1.3. 短文閱讀（短文阅读）： Wang Hong has written the journal entry below after doing some investigation into endangered species in her own city. This is an opinion piece that also cites some research and objective statistics. In the following form, sort out the objective facts from the personal opinions.

瀕臨絕種的野生動物並不僅止於一些獨特的動物，如非洲的大象、中國特有的大熊貓、印度的老虎等等。我們熟悉的家鄉也有相當多瀕臨絕種的動物以及植物。據統計，全球八千多種植物以及七千多種動物目前都瀕臨絕種。它們日益減少的原因，除了環境污染、棲息地縮小之外，還有，獵人為了它們的商業價值而捕殺這些動物或濫採植物，比如象牙、老虎皮等等。我們都有保護動物的責任，但有時一個人的理想和慾望會發生衝突：我們既想保護環境，又想買那些產品或者開發溼地和森林。發生衝突的時候，我們必須提醒自己，人類和這些動植物的生命是息息相關的。

瀕临绝种的野生动物并不仅止于一些独特的动物，如非洲的大象、中国特有的大熊猫、印度的老虎等等。我们熟悉的家乡也有相当多瀕临绝种的动物以及植物。据统计，全球八千多种植物以及七千多种动物目前都瀕临绝种。它们日益减少的原因，除了环境污染、栖息地缩小之外，还有，猎人为了它们的商业价值而捕杀这些动物或滥采植物，比如象牙、老虎皮等等。我们都有保护动物的责任，但有时一个人的理想和欲望会发生冲突：我们既想保护环境，又想买那些产品或者开发湿地和森林。发生冲突的时候，我们必须提醒自己，人类和这些动植物的生命是息息相关的。

Objective Facts	Personal Opinions

16.1.4. 口語回答（口语回答）： You are running for the position of president of your school's Animal Protection Club; this is a simulation of an interview for the position by other members of the club. Each time it is your turn to speak, you have twenty seconds to record your response. You should respond as fully and as appropriately as possible. There will be six times when it is your turn to speak.

16.1.5. 課堂口語活動（课堂口语活动）

A. 小海龜回大海（小海龟回大海）： Describe the story you see in the following pictures.

B. Choose an endangered plant or animal species not described in section 16.1.3 and give a report about its numbers, habitat, endangered status, and other important information. Enhance your report with photographs, tables, charts, and other visual aids.

16.1.6. 寫作（写作）

A. 動物是人類的朋友（动物是人类的朋友）

Write a story of the friendship between an animal and a human being. It can be your own experience with your pet or a story that you have read or heard.

B. 我最喜歡的野生動物（我最喜欢的野生动物）

Write a short paragraph telling about your favorite wild animal, one that may or may not be endangered. You need to do some research to find out the answers to the following questions related to the animal that you choose. Be sure to cite your sources. Compare your findings to your initial impressions.

a. 描述這種動物生活的自然生態環境，這種動物是否瀕臨絕種？
   描述这种动物生活的自然生态环境，这种动物是否濒临绝种？

b. 牠在不同季節有不同的繁殖地和棲息地嗎？
   它在不同季节有不同的繁殖地和栖息地吗？

c. 牠的棲息地有沒有受到破壞或縮小？
   它的栖息地有没有受到破坏或缩小？

d. 這種動物在野外的數量有多少？
   这种动物在野外的数量有多少？

e. 這種動物是否有商業價值？什麼樣的價值？
   这种动物是否有商业价值？什么样的价值？

f. 獵人捕殺這種動物是否合法？
   猎人捕杀这种动物是否合法？

16.2. 關心大熊貓，關心人類自己（关心大熊猫，关心人类自己）

16.2.1. 生詞練習（生词练习）

A. 解釋生詞（解释生词）：a to **j** are definitions for the words in the box. Find and fill in an appropriate word from the list for each definition.

分散，物品，捐，嚴重，管道，資源，失去，兩全其美，面臨，不斷
分散，物品，捐，严重，管道，资源，失去，两全其美，面临，不断

a. _____ 本來擁有的，後來沒有了
本来拥有，后来没有了

b. _____ 天然資源，比如：水，石油等
天然资源，比如：水，石油等

c. _____ 一種情況或辦法，讓對立的兩方面都有好處
一种情况或办法，让对立的两方面都有好处

d. _____ 把錢和物品送給需要的人或者機構
把钱和物品送给需要的人或者机构

e. _____ 連續不停（连续不停）

f. _____ 程度深，影響大（程度深，影响大）

g. _____ 不集中，在各處都有（不集中，在各处都有）

h. _____ 途徑，門路，方式（途径，门路，方式）

i. _____ 面對問題、情況等（面对问题、情况等）

j. _____ 日常生活中用的東西（日常生活中用的东西）

B. 填空: Shufen is providing some information on bamboo for her classmates. Fill in the blanks in the following passage with words in the box.

製成，植物，農產品，種類
制成，植物，农产品，种类

竹子可以長得又高又大，很多人以為竹子跟大樹一樣，事實上，根據_____學的分類，竹子是一種草而不是樹。中國的竹子_____繁多，功能也不計其數。竹子跟中國人的生活息息相關，竹子可用來蓋房子，_____家具、筷子、樂器。竹子的幼苗也是一種_____，竹筍是可以吃的菜！

★★★★★

竹子可以长得又高又大，很多人以为竹子跟大树一样，事实上，根据_____学的分类，竹子是一种草而不是树。中国的竹子_____繁多，功能也不计其数。竹子跟中国人的生活息息相关，竹子可用来盖房子，_____家具、筷子、乐器。竹子的幼苗也是一种_____，竹笋是可以吃的菜！

C. 填空: The following is a brief report of the current state of pandas in China. Choose an appropriate word from the top list to complete the following passage.

| 其中，廣 ，體重，導致， 設立，面臨，立法，相當於 |
| 其中， 广 ，体重，导致， 设立， 面临， 立法， 相当于 |

　　小熊貓很可愛，而成年大熊貓的＿＿＿＿＿＿常在 99 到 149 公斤之間，＿＿＿＿＿＿220 到 330 磅。兩、三萬年前大熊貓分佈的範圍很＿＿＿＿＿，但由於人類不斷地使大熊貓的棲息和繁殖地縮小，＿＿＿＿＿＿今日只有四川省和甘肅省才有野生大熊貓，而且正＿＿＿＿＿絕種的問題。為了保護熊貓，中國＿＿＿＿＿＿了 60 個大熊貓保護區，＿＿＿＿＿＿以臥龍區為最大，最有名。為了保護臥龍區的大熊貓，中國政府已經＿＿＿＿＿＿禁止在當地狩獵和砍伐樹木。

★ ★ ★ ★ ★

　　小熊猫很可爱，而成年大熊猫的＿＿＿＿＿＿常在 99 到 149 公斤之间，＿＿＿＿＿＿220 到 330 磅。两、三万年前大熊猫分布的范围很＿＿＿＿＿，但由于人类不断地使大熊猫的栖息和繁殖地缩小，＿＿＿＿＿＿今日只有四川省和甘肃省才有野生大熊猫，而且正＿＿＿＿＿绝种的问题。为了保护熊猫，中国＿＿＿＿＿＿了 60 个大熊猫保护区，＿＿＿＿＿＿以卧龙区为最大，最有名。为了保护卧龙区的大熊猫，中国政府已经＿＿＿＿＿＿禁止在当地狩猎和砍伐树木。

D. 是威脅還是保護？（是威胁还是保护？）: Do the following items describe threats to the survival of the Giant Panda or efforts toward protecting them?　Write either 威脅 or 保護 (威胁 or 保护) next to each item.

a. 種群分散(种群分散)_____　　i. 認養(认养)_____

b. 捐錢(捐钱)_____　　　　　　j. 森林大火_____

c. 狩獵(狩猎)_____　　　　　　k. 設立保護區
　　　　　　　　　　　　　　　　　 设立保护区_____

d. 節約資源(节约资源)_____

e. 砍伐_____　　　　　　　　　l. 購買利用瀕臨絕種的動物所製
　　　　　　　　　　　　　　　　　 成的物品

f. 竹子開花(竹子开花)_____　　　 购买利用濒临绝种的动物所制
　　　　　　　　　　　　　　　　　 成的物品

g. 減少污染(减少污染)_____　　　 _____

h. 立法_____

16.2.2. 聽力（听力）

A. You and your friend Long En want to join the Animal Protection Club on campus this semester.　You both plan to attend the first meeting this afternoon.　Unfortunately, Long En got sick and did not come to school.　He wants you to send him an e-mail summarizing the main points of what the president of the club, Zhu Tiansheng, said at the meeting.

B. Listen to the conversations and complete the rejoinders. You will hear two short conversations or parts of conversations followed by four choices, designated (A), (B), (C), and (D). Choose the one that continues or completes the conversation in a logical and culturally appropriate manner.

1. (　　) 2. (　　)

16.2.3. 短文閱讀（短文阅读）： The following is a piece of news posted by the Animal Protection Club in the campus newspaper. Read the passage and then answer the questions.

> 　　十月四日是「世界動物日」，全世界都在這一天舉辦很多慶祝活動來感謝人類的朋友--可愛的動物們。「世界動物日」是 1931 年由一個義大利生態學會的科學家正式訂立的。　選擇十月四日這天是源自十九世紀一位義大利修道士弗朗西的倡議。他熱愛動物，要求村民們在十月四日這天「獻愛心給動物」。「世界動物日」的網站 http://www.worldanimalday.org.uk/index.asp 是 2003 年建立的。我們學校的動物保護社打算在那天辦一個照片展覽，展示我們居住地區正瀕臨絕種的動物的照片，以及提供保護動物的方式和管道。
>
>
>
> 　　十月四日是"世界动物日"，全世界都在这一天举办很多庆祝活动来感谢人类的朋友--可爱的动物们。"世界动物日"是 1931 年由一个意大利生态学会的科学家正式订立的。　选择十月四日这天是源自十九世纪一位意大利修道士弗朗西的倡议。他热爱动物，要求村民们在十月四日这天"献爱心给动物"。"世界动物日"的网站 http://www.worldanimalday.org.uk/index.asp 是 2003 年建立的。我们学校的动物保护社打算在那天办一个照片展览，展示我们居住地区正濒临绝种的动物的照片，以及提供保护动物的方式和管道。

a. When was World Animal Day officially established?
1) 2003
2) 1931
3) the nineteenth century
4) the early twentieth century

b. What event will be held in the school to celebrate World Animal Day?
1) The club will exhibit photos of endangered animals from around the world.
2) The club will provide information on methods for taking care of pets.
3) The club will highlight the local animal species that are endangered.
4) The club will express students' love for animals through posters.

16.2.4. 實文閱讀（实文阅读）： Choose the appropriate answers for the following multiple-choice questions, based on the flyer below.

國際環保日比賽
主題：我們只有一個地球

比賽組別：國中組，高中組，大學組

比賽詳情：

1. 參加者須提交一份推廣校內環保的活動計劃書。活動計劃的預算開支不可多於 1000 元新臺幣。
2. 每所學校提名學生組成隊伍參賽。每隊由 7 至 10 名學生組成。參加者須填妥報名表，並於四月二十二日（星期五）或之前傳真至環保會秘書辦公室。
3. 得獎公布日期：五月十八日，每個入圍隊伍將會獲頒獎金以推行其校內的環保活動計劃。
4. 收件時間：即日起至四月二十二日止
5. 收件地址：高雄市大同區三民路 302 號 5 樓

歡迎踴躍參加！

国际环保日比赛
主题：我们只有一个地球

比赛组别：国中组，高中组，大学组

比赛详情：

1. 参加者须提交一份推广校内环保的活动计划书。活动计划的预算开支不可多于 1000 元新台币。
2. 每所学校提名学生组成队伍参赛。每队由 7 至 10 名学生组成。参加者须填妥报名表，并于四月二十二日（星期五）或之前传真至环保会秘书办公室。
3. 得奖公布日期：五月十八日，每个入围队伍将会获颁奖金以推行其校内的环保活动计划。
4. 收件时间：即日起至四月二十二日止
5. 收件地址：高雄市大同区三民路 302 号 5 楼

欢迎踊跃参加！

---

a. What kind of activity is being promoted in this flyer?
   1) a contest for designing activities for Earth Day in schools
   2) a contest on knowledge of environmental protection
   3) a contest for proposals to improve the environment on campus
   4) a contest for raising funds for environmental protection

b. The winners will
   1) be provided funding to implement their plan.
   2) present their work on World Environment Day.
   3) be presented trophies at City Hall.
   4) be notified on 22 April.

16.2.5. 課堂口語活動（课堂口语活动）

A. Have you participated in fund-raising? Think of something that is meaningful to you for which you could organize a fund-raising event, and give a short persuasive speech to your classmates to convince them to participate. Tell them how the money would be raised, what tasks you need people to take on, and what good would come of it.

B. You are thinking about studying abroad in China with the opportunity of working on some kind of volunteer job. Put together an outline of a trip to China for yourself where service learning is an important component. Present your itinerary and a description of the service learning activity or program that you choose; tell your classmates about the activity or program, why you made this choice, the amount of time that would be spent in various locales doing various activities, and what you would learn from the experience.

C. The tension between conservation and economic development isn't unique to Wolong; it is pervasive. What are your thoughts about finding ways to accommodate both? Work with one or more classmates to role-play a discussion among different stakeholders in a particular area; include viewpoints from conservationists, local residents, developers, government representatives, and others you think important. Be specific about the locale, with relevant species and economic issues. You can focus on areas in China or somewhere in your local area.

16.2.6. 看圖寫作（看图写作）： The four pictures tell a story. Imagine you are reporting the story to a friend. Write down the complete story as suggested by the pictures. Give your story a beginning, a middle part, and an end.

16.2.7. 寫作（写作）

A. Write a letter that could be shared with students at Wolong or other panda reserves in China, telling them about an endangered species in your country, why it is endangered, and how people are working to protect it; tell them what you've learned about the Giant Panda, and ask them what you'd like to know about the students' lives to better understand the issues involved with protecting pandas.

B. Based on your experience with the role-play in 16.2.5.C in the workbook, discuss the tensions between economic development and environmentalism, as well as solutions to these tensions. Again, base your arguments on a specific locale with its particular resources, species, and issues. Find information from at least two sources, and be sure to cite them.

第十七課　　我們只有一個地球
第十七课　　我们只有一个地球

17.1.環境污染（环境污染）

17.1.1. 生詞練習（生词练习）

A. From the box, choose and list the items that pertain to the questions.

> 沙漠，電池，樹木，垃圾，廢氣，濕地，塑膠袋，水土，工業
> 沙漠，电池，树木，垃圾，废气，湿地，塑胶袋，水土，工业

　　a. 哪些是人為的?_____, _____, _____, _____, _____

　　b. 哪些是天然的（不是人為的）?

　　　_____, _____, _____, _____

B. 連連看（连连看）: Match the words on the left with the appropriate definition on the right.

　　a. 地球　　　　　　按照種類把東西分開（按照种类把东西分开）

　　b. 海報（海报）　　不能再用的水

　　c. 一般　　　　　　少用,不浪費東西（少用,不浪费东西）

　　d. 能源　　　　　　重新再使用一樣東西（重新再使用一样东西）

　　e. 節約（节约）　　水,風,石油這些東西（水,风,石油这些东西）

　　f. 宣傳（宣传）　　人類住的地方（人类住的地方）

　　g. 廢水（废水）　　對一件事或情況產生的討厭的感覺
　　　　　　　　　　　　对一件事或情况产生的讨厌的感觉

　　h. 回收　　　　　　沒什麼特別的（没什么特别的）

　　i. 分類（分类）　　抽這東西對健康有害（抽这东西对健康有害）

　　j. 香煙（香烟）　　用來宣傳的一種工具（用来宣传的一种工具）

　　k. 可惡（可恶）　　用不同的法子告訴很多人一件事
　　　　　　　　　　　　用不同的法子告诉很多人一件事

C. 簡答題：簡單回答下面問題
簡答題：简单回答下面问题

a. 請舉出兩個你節省能源的方法？
   请举出两个你节省能源的方法？

b. 你家或者學校做資源回收的工作嗎？請舉出兩個例子。
   你家或者学校做资源回收的工作吗？请举出两个例子。

c. 為什麼使用永續能源可以保護環境？
   为什么使用永续能源可以保护环境？

d. 如果過度砍伐森林的樹木會對環境造成什麼破壞？
   如果过度砍伐森林的树木会对环境造成什么破坏？

e. 推動垃圾分類有什麼方法？請舉兩個例子。
   推动垃圾分类有什么方法？请举两个例子。

17.1.2. 聽力（听力）: Listen to the conversations and complete the rejoinders. You will hear two short conversations or parts of conversations followed by four choices, designated (A), (B), (C), and (D). Choose the one that continues or completes the conversation in a logical and culturally appropriate manner.

1. (　　)　　2. (　　)

17.1.3. 短文閱讀（短文阅读）: Meifen and Mingdao discuss their opinions on environmental protection. Check the correct answers after reading their statements.

美芬的意見

　　我認為，為了人類的後代子孫，我們應該從小就提高孩子保護地球的意識，也就是「保護地球，人人有責」，還應養成孩子節約能源的習慣。比方說，節約用水、少用電、不用塑膠袋，還有多走路、少開車、多用可以回收的東西等等，這些日常生活上的小事都是很容易做到的。

明道的意見

　　科學家總是發表一些研究報告，說什麼地球溫度上升了，北極冰山要融化了。我個人對這些專家提供的科學訊息還是抱著非常謹慎的態度。我覺得地球已經存在了幾億年了，不可能只因為一些工業發展就消失。我們是地球上最聰明的動物，應該過著最方便的生活。保護環境的團體一天到晚要我們少用這個、不用那個、這個不好、那個不行，這樣的生活還有什麼意思呢？

★ ★ ★ ★ ★

美芬的意见

　　我认为，为了人类的后代子孙，我们应该从小就提高孩子保护地球的意识，也就是"保护地球，人人有责"，还应养成孩子节约能源的习惯。比方说，节约用水、少用电、不用塑料袋，还有多走路、少开车、多用可以回收的东西等等，这些日常生活上的小事都是很容易做到的。

明道的意见

　　科学家总是发表一些研究报告，说什么地球温度上升了，北极冰山要融化了。可是我个人对这些专家提供的科学讯息还是抱着非常谨慎的态度。我觉得地球已经存在了几亿年了，不可能只因为一些工业发展就消失。我们是地球上最聪明的动物，应该过着最方便的生活。　保护环境的团体一天到晚要我们少用这个、不用那个、这个不好、那个不行，这样的生活还有什么意思呢？

Who is more likely to do the following things?

	美芬	明道
a. Buy an SUV.	☐	☐
b. Bring a shopping bag.	☐	☐
c. Educate kids to save energy.	☐	☐
d. Take a bubble bath.	☐	☐
e. Go on a shopping spree.	☐	☐
f. Walk to school.	☐	☐
g. Question scientific research.	☐	☐
h. Use recycled products.	☐	☐

17.1.4. 口語回答（口语回答）： You want to volunteer at the Environmental Center in your community. You will participate in a simulated interview with the interviewer from the center. Each time it is your turn to speak, you have twenty seconds to record your response. You should respond as fully and as appropriately as possible. There will be six times when it is your turn to speak.

17.1.5. 課堂口語活動（课堂口语活动）

A. 看圖說話（看图说话）：請勿吸煙（请勿吸烟）

B. 州内、市區的環保工作（州内、市区的环保工作）： To enhance understanding of the status of environmental issues where you live, your class decides to find out what environmental tasks have been done or have been ignored in your city or at the state level. Divide the class into small groups. Each group does research and collects data for a specific project launched or for an area that needs attention. For example, if you live in Texas, you may find the information that voters supported a bill to provide funding to protect the state parks in November 2007. Since then, several plans have been launched to clean the water and air in the parks. Report your group's findings to the whole class, demonstrating important data on posters or PowerPoint slides.

17.1.6. 寫作（写作）

A. You read Meifen's and Mingdao's opinions in the reading assignment in 17.1.3. Write a paragraph explaining your reaction to their opinions and your position with respect to environmental protection.

B. Imagine you are a visitor from Mars and are surprised at the pollution on the planet Earth. You had heard about beautiful Earth but what you see is totally different. Is it reversible? Write a paragraph offering your generous advice to the human inhabitants so that Earth can be saved.

17.2. 改善社區環境（改善社区环境）

17.2.1. 生詞練習（生词练习）

A. 近義詞還是相反詞？（近义词还是相反词？）： Write S or A to indicate whether each of the following pairs are synonyms or antonyms. For example, the pair in **a** are synonyms.

a. 一般	普通	S	j. 植物（植物）	樹木（树木）	___
b. 偏僻	熱鬧（热闹）	___	k. 節省（节省）	浪費（浪费）	___
c. 享受	喜歡（喜欢）	___	l. 原來（原来）	本來（本来）	___
d. 停止	帶動（带动）	___	m. 宣傳（宣传）	廣告（广告）	___
e. 改善	進步（进步）	___	n. 推動（推动）	實行（实行）	___
f. 步行	走路	___	o. 悠閒（悠闲）	緊張（紧张）	___
g. 居民	遊客（游客）	___			
h. 浪漫	嚴肅（严肃）	___			
i. 上升	提高	___			

B. 社區環境（社区环境）： List five neighborhood activities in which you are frequently engaged, and five activities that you would like to see available.

我們的社區從事的活動 我们的社区从事的活动	希望我們的社區能從事的活動 希望我们的社区能从事的活动

C. 填空： Mr. Wang, a realtor, is persuading his clients Mr. and Mrs. Li to purchase a house in a newly developed neighborhood. Use the words in the box to fill in the blanks in the following paragraph.

> 改善，享受，悠閒，景觀，偏僻，浪漫
>
> 改善，享受，悠闲，景观，偏僻，浪漫

這裡是這附近最新開發的社區，幾年前這一帶還是一片原始的森林地帶，位置_____，一條公路都沒有。現在，您看，所有的_____完全不一樣了，交通條件也_____了不少。要是在這個社區居住，您就可以每天_____這裡的大自然，可以和家人一起在林間小道_____地散步，忘掉所有生活上的煩惱。您說，這是不是最_____的住家環境啊！

★ ★ ★ ★ ★

这里是这附近最新开发的社区，几年前这一带还是一片原始的森林地带，位置_____，一条公路都没有。现在，您看，所有的_____完全不一样了，交通条件也_____了不少。要是在这个社区居住，您就可以每天_____这里的大自然，可以和家人一起在林间小道_____地散步，忘掉所有生活上的烦恼。您说，这是不是最_____的住家环境啊！

D. 填空： Mr. and Mrs. Li, the potential home buyers, are talking about the newly developed neighborhood shown by Mr. Wang. Use the words in the box to fill in the blanks in the following paragraph.

改善，享受，悠閒，景觀，偏僻，浪漫
改善，享受，悠闲，景观，偏僻，浪漫

李先生： 你覺得今天上午看的那個房子怎麼樣？

李太太： 你說的是那個新開發的森林社區嗎？好是好，就是太_____了一點，路也不太好，恐怕進出不太方便。你看以後會_____嗎？

李先生： 我倒看不出有麼不方便的，那兒的_____那麼好，連開車都有_____的感覺。

李太太： 你這個人，真是太_____了，怎麼連開車都覺得是一種_____啊？我真不懂。

李先生： 別擔心了，我的好太太。我們明天開車過去再好好看看。

★★★★★

李先生： 你觉得今天上午看的那个房子怎么样？

李太太： 你说的是那个新开发的森林社区吗？好是好，就是太_____了一点，路也不太好，恐怕进出不太方便。你看以后会_____吗？

李先生： 我倒看不出有么不方便的，那儿的_____那么好，连开车都有_____的感觉。

李太太： 你这个人，真是太_____了，怎么连开车都觉得是一种_____啊？我真不懂。

李先生： 别担心了，我的好太太。我们明天开车过去再好好看看。

17.2.2. 聽力(听力)

A. You will hear an announcement made in a park tour bus regarding the park regulations. Listen to the recording and answer the following true or false questions based on what you hear.

對(对)	錯(错)		
❑	❑	1.	This is an ecological park.
❑	❑	2.	This park features wildlife.
❑	❑	3.	There are designated areas for smoking.
❑	❑	4.	There are designated areas for food and beverages.
❑	❑	5.	Visitors can freely ramble in the park.
❑	❑	6.	The park administration urges visitors to engage in environmental protection for the sake of everyone.

B. Listen to the conversations and complete the rejoinders. You will hear two short conversations or parts of conversations followed by four choices, designated (A), (B), (C), and (D). Choose the one that continues or completes the conversation in a logical and culturally appropriate manner.

　　　1. (　) 　2. (　　)

17.2.3. 短文閱讀（短文阅读）: In a blog, Lin Liling shared her sentiments about a recent experience. Based on her blog, answer the following multiple-choice questions.

人類，請少製造垃圾，多保護環境

　　經過了幾個小時辛苦的工作，我和班上的同學利用週末終於把一小段公路兩旁的垃圾清理乾淨了，這個地方又回到了原本的自然景觀。為什麼公路兩旁有那麼多的垃圾，難道丟垃圾的人不知道破壞地球就是害自己？我真希望再也沒有人隨便丟垃圾。每一個地球人都應該少製造垃圾，多保護環境，讓大家都能享受綠色家園。只要在日常生活中，每個人都少用一張紙、少抽一根煙、少用一個塑膠袋、少用一雙免洗筷吃飯、少扔掉一顆電池、多種一棵樹、多走一段路，我們的地球就會越來越健康，我們的生活就會越來越快樂。

　　保護環境，人人有責。我要大聲說：「人類，請少製造垃圾，多保護環境。」讓我們好好愛護我們的地球母親吧！

★ ★ ★ ★ ★

人类，请少制造垃圾，多保护环境

经过了几个小时辛苦的工作，我和班上的同学利用周末终于把一小段公路两旁的垃圾清理干净了，这个地方又回到了原本的自然景观。为什么公路两旁有那么多的垃圾，难道丢垃圾的人不知道破坏地球就是害自己？我真希望再也没有人随便丢垃圾。每一个地球人都应该少制造垃圾，多保护环境，让大家都能享受绿色家园。只要在日常生活中，每个人少用一张纸、少抽一根烟、少用一个塑胶袋、少用一双免洗筷吃饭、少扔掉一颗电池、多种一棵树、多走一段路，我们的地球就会越来越健康，我们的生活就会越来越快乐。

保护环境，人人有责。我要大声说："人类，请少制造垃圾，多保护环境。"让我们好好爱护我们的地球母亲吧！

1. What is the main purpose of Lin Liling's blog?
    a. To urge people to join her environmental team.
    b. To report to the class about her service project.
    c. To advocate the importance of buying recycled products.
    d. To reflect her thoughts about doing weekend service.

2. What did Lin Liling do on the weekend?
    a. Collected garbage along the road.
    b. Planted trees near the highway.
    c. Made signs to promote environmental protection.
    d. Educated tourists to keep the park clean.

3. What does Lin Liling ask people to do?
    a. Plant more trees.
    b. Smoke cigarettes outdoors more often.
    c. Use disposable chopsticks more often.
    d. Use batteries less often.

4. What did Lin Liling equate the earth to?
    a. father
    b. mother
    c. home
    d. paradise

17.2.4. 實文閱讀（实文阅读）

筷行動！
保護綠色森林
不使用一次性筷子

當您使用一次性筷子的一刹那，又為伐木人找到一個破壞森林的理由。森林的消失所帶來的水土流失、沙塵暴以及動物的流離失所將是您流傳給子孫的禮物。

筷行动！
保护绿色森林
不使用一次性筷子

当您使用一次性筷子的一刹那，又为伐木人找到一个破坏森林的理由。森林的消失所带来的水土流失、沙尘暴以及动物的流离失所将是您流传给子孙的礼物。

Choose an appropriate answer for each question, based on the authentic material above.

1. What is the main message put forth in the ad?
   a. stopping water pollution
   b. preventing deforestation
   c. protecting the environment as a gift for future generations
   d. the outcome of using disposable chopsticks

2. What kind of professional is mentioned in the ad?
   a. chef   b. geologist   c. lumberjack   d. meteorologist

3. What "gift" is not mentioned in the ad?
   a. sand   b. mud   c. snow   d. animals

17.2.5. 課堂口語活動（课堂口语活动）

A. China is holding a national contest for the best poster promoting environmental protection. Your class plans to participate in the contest. Divide the class into small groups. Each group does research on an area of environmental pollution or destruction in China, as well as a poster that can urge people to protect the environment. Each group will present their findings and poster in class: report the problems, suggest possible improvements, and demonstrate the group poster.

B. Your sister high school in China will start a campaign for environmental awareness and develop several activities to clean up the campus and the community. Students there ask for suggestions from your class. Divide the class into small groups. Each group plans a feasible and effective activity that raises awareness of the need to protect the environment and improve the environment in your campus and community, based on your research of some successful projects. Each group presents their activity in class.

17.2.6. 看圖寫作（看图写作）:
The four pictures tell a story. Imagine you are reporting a story to a friend. Write down the complete story as suggested by the pictures. Give your story a beginning, a middle part, and an end.

17.2.7. 寫作（写作）

A. You read Lin Liling's blog in 17.2.3 regarding environmental protection. Write a response to her blog and share your own experience in and thoughts about environmental protection.

B. You were an exchange student in Xi'an, China, for a semester last year. You had a memorable time, except for one thing: you could not avoid smokers anyplace you went. In order to express your concern, you start a blog in Chinese. In the introduction of the blog, you provide the example of the United States. How did Americans change their perception of smoking? How did Americans refuse to inhale secondhand smoke? What policies were established to prohibit smokers in public spaces, such as restaurants, movie theaters, and offices? Of course, in the blog, you should encourage readers to send their responses and comments.